THE AUTHOR
Kevin Walker

Kevin Walker lives in the Brecon Beacons area of mid Wales, and has been a professional mountain leader and hill guide for almost four decades. A self-confessed mountain addict, he ran ML training courses for several years, and has written many books including *Mountain Hazards*, *Wild Country Camping*, *The Essential Hillwalkers' Guide*, and *Undiscovered Wales*.

He runs a wide range of navigation, hill skills and mountaincraft courses, as well as offering personal tuition, 1:1 coaching, and private guiding. Further details of the courses and walking events are available on his web site at www.mountain-activities.com, where you can also check availability, make online bookings, and buy books and guides.

When not teaching or guiding, he spends most of his free time exploring, photographing and writing about the less well known parts of Wales, with occasional trips to further flung hills, most recently the Spanish Sierras de Tejeda and the Nepal Himalayas.

ACKNOWLEDGEMENTS

This book would not have been possible without the help and companionship of many people, including all those who have attended my navigation and hill skills courses over the years. Teaching is undoubtedly the best way to learn!

More especially, I would like to acknowledge the immense help and support that I have received from the many colleagues with whom I have worked (and played) on the hills. I count the camaraderie and our shared experiences amongst my most valued possessions.

Mention too must be made of my publisher Franco and his great team of editors and designers, who have made the process of turning my rough draft into a proper book easy and painless!

To all those whom I have mentioned, my grateful thanks – to any I have neglected, my humble apologies.

CONTENTS

MAPS

INTRODUCTION

"GOOD NAVIGATORS ARE NEVER LOST ...
BUT THEY MAY BE 'LOCATIONALLY CHALLENGED'!"

Navigation is a major part of the wider art of mountaincraft and, as such, should be regarded as an essential component skill rather than the be-all and end-all of a day in the wild. I firmly believe that understanding this basic concept is vital to successful wilderness navigation. Put simply, it means that if you are a skilled navigator, you do not need to know *precisely* where you are all the time (although you will usually have a reasonable idea), because you have both the ability and the confidence to work out where you are when needed. This is a tremendous asset, for it affords you the freedom of the hills.

If you find you are a slave to your navigation, spending much of your time walking around with map in hand, trying to keep your thumb over your precise position, constantly consulting your compass and counting paces and minutes, then you are definitely doing it all wrong. Successful navigation should be simple and straightforward, and when done correctly, it will enhance the pleasure you get from the great outdoors, not detract from it.

I have now been running navigation courses for well over thirty years, and this book is based largely on my experiences. What I have come to realise is that the most common barrier to learning and understanding is a mistaken preconception; people think navigation is difficult, so they make it difficult. When attending my navigation courses, most people's expectations are that they are going to find it complicated, so when they wander across the moors and find that navigating is actually simple, they look worried and ask what they are doing wrong!

Although map interpretation, and more especially some of the poor visibility techniques, may appear complicated, they are actually quite straightforward. As long as you can get to grips with a few basic principles you will find that this type of navigation is easy. The best way to learn is to take it step by step, gaining as much familiarity, understanding and experience as possible of each stage, before progressing to the next.

There is a common misconception that we should correct at an early stage. When presented with a map and a compass and asked to select the most important tool for successful navigation, most people choose the compass. Unfortunately, this is totally wrong! Even if you are the best compass navigator in the world, able to follow bearings within incredible precision it means nothing unless you can relate the bearing to a map. It is simply an invisible line that goes from somewhere to somewhere else – possibly through a bog and over the top of a cliff! Over-use of the compass combined with under-use of map interpretation is an extremely common error, even amongst experienced hillwalkers. Indeed, it is one of the most common reasons that candidates fail when being assessed for National Governing Body qualifications.

In reality, map interpretation should account for a good 90% of your navigation. Of the remaining 10%, compass work will account for about 6%, and estimating time and distance, the remaining 4%. With practice and experience, you should be able to read a map like a book; one which gives you such a complete and accurate picture of your surroundings that, for the vast majority of the time, there will be no need for you to use any other equipment or techniques.

I have tried to write this book in such a way that it allows you to follow a structured course of learning. Based loosely on my first navigation book (*Mountain Navigation Techniques*, Constable, 1986) and its subsequent reincarnations, I have completely revised and updated the original text, and have made much use of the experiences I have gained over many years whilst running navigation courses at all levels from total novice to aspirant instructor. In Part One, we look at maps, mapping and map interpretation, and how you can use your map to give you a detailed picture of the terrain. Part Two is concerned with compasses and bearings, and how you can use simple techniques to give you a precise measure of direction in even the thickest mist. In Part Three we examine a whole range of additional techniques that will be of particular use in poor visibility or when crossing featureless or difficult terrain, including how to estimate time and distance with great accuracy, and how to 'tweak' your bearings to make life simple. We also discuss the advantages and disadvantages of route cards, look at a few difficult situations, and introduce the somewhat thorny subject of GPS devices and smart phone apps. Last but by no means least, in Part Four we cover what I believe to be the real core of navigation – the art of relocation – or how to work out where you are when you are 'locationally challenged'. The reason this is left to the end is that it relies heavily on a reasonable familiarity with all the other techniques.

If you are new to navigation, there are a few technical terms which may be confusing. To help make things clearer, the first time such 'jargon' is used I have shown it in **bold**, and many of these terms are then explained further in the glossary at the back of the book.

There is one point that must be stressed right from the start; simply sitting down and absorbing all the information in this book will not, in itself, make you a good navigator. Without practical experience you will still be next to useless when it comes to navigating in the sort of conditions where your life, and perhaps the lives of others in your group, depend on your accuracy.

Use every opportunity you can to gain as much experience as possible of all the techniques, particularly map interpretation, and continue practising them regularly. Your ultimate aim should be to become so familiar with the basic techniques that they are second nature. When walking as a member of a group, stop relying on someone else to do all the navigation, and offer to help or even to lead part of the walk yourself. When you are a passenger in a car, have a 1:50,000 scale map handy, and try to work out what is coming up ahead, not just in terms of the road configuration, but more in terms of the terrain and the general shape of the land. Use a 1:25,000 scale map to plan short walks near your home; work out what you think you are going to see, then go out and check how right you were. Who knows? You may even find out something about your neighbourhood which you had never realised before. Indeed, there are countless things you can do, even if you live in the middle of a city; and if, at this early stage, it all starts to become a little tedious – stop! Do something else for a while and then come back to it. Navigation should be, and can be, fun!

PART 1 – THE MAP

Map reading and, more specifically, map interpretation should make up at least 90% of your navigation, so it makes sense to start by looking at maps and mapping, and to investigate how you can use map interpretation techniques to get an incredibly detailed picture of the terrain. We will look at the differences between map reading and map interpretation in more detail later. For the time being, suffice it to say that the one thing that separates the good navigator from the not-so-good is the ability to interpret the map. This being so, the map is unquestionably the most important tool you have, so it makes sense that you should know exactly what you are using. So what is a map?

1 WHAT IS A MAP?

This is one of the first questions I ask people who come on my navigation courses. Although it is an outwardly simple question, it often results in surprisingly puzzled expressions. Of course, we all know – to a greater or lesser extent – what a map is, but actually putting this into words seems to cause problems. The most common answer is along the lines of, "a map is a two dimensional representation of a three dimensional landscape". Well, yes it is – but is this not a good example of how people tend to look at navigation in an overly complicated way? Would it not be much easier to think of a map simply as a picture?

For our purposes, the best way to think of a map is as a picture of the ground taken from vertically above. Indeed, aerial photography and satellite imagery play a crucial part in the making of modern maps, and this is particularly true in rural areas. However, there is a problem; whilst many people will be familiar with vertical aerial or satellite photographs, most will also recognise how confusing they can be. Different features tend to merge with one another, and unless the sun is low on the horizon, thus casting long shadows, the whole landscape can look totally flat and bland. Additionally, even after quite detailed examination, it is often extremely difficult to decide whether the large green square is a field of cabbages or a coniferous plantation, or whether the obvious, sinuous line is a stream, a path or a hedge. It is also very difficult to get any realistic impression of distance or scale without having an obvious point of reference.

The job of a modern cartographer is to take these aerial photographs and satellite images, to merge the information thus gained with the results of a variety of surveys (assuming, of course, that such surveys are available – which may not be the case in more remote areas), and to convert all this data into a clear and usable picture of the ground. In order to be of any practical use, this must be an accurate picture, which shows as many of the features as possible (all in their exact relative positions), tells you what is high and what is low and how steeply the ground slopes in between, and allows you to see, at a glance, the relative distances and sizes.

In an attempt to make things even clearer for us, cartographers use a set of symbols called **conventional signs** to represent the various objects and features that might otherwise be ambiguous or difficult to interpret. The problems of showing height and slope have been solved by the use of **contour lines**, and the difficulties of showing distance and size have been overcome by drawing the map according to a particular ratio or scale.

To recap

A map is a simply picture of the ground drawn in such a way that it gives a clear and accurate description of the landscape and features. The better the map, the clearer and more accurate it will be.

2 TYPES OF MAP

Maps come in many different shapes, sizes and formats, only a few of which are suitable for use when travelling through mountain and moorland landscapes. To give an extreme example, a road map may be useful when driving between Dartmoor and the Cairngorms, but it will be of limited use when walking across either place in misty conditions.

The types of map most suitable for our purposes are those that display detailed and accurate landscape information in a way that is readily accessible and easily understood. There are currently two different makes of map available in the United Kingdom which possess all the necessary qualities, these being Ordnance Survey (OS) maps and BMC/Harvey maps. Both types have advantages and disadvantages.

Ordnance Survey (OS) maps are very accurate and extremely detailed. However, as we will see later, they are not always user-friendly so far as walkers and climbers are concerned, simply because they are so accurate and detailed! The problem is that they contain a whole host of information which is next to useless for mountain and moorland navigation because it does not appear on the ground – boundaries being just one case in point – and this information can obscure the more important stuff that is of use. Additionally, on both the Explorer and Landranger series, several types of landscape feature are shown as general portrayals rather than specific features, and this can cause problems in complex, rocky areas where the contour lines may be difficult to read or even obscured.

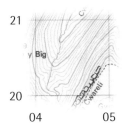

1:50,000 Ordnance
Survey Landranger 160

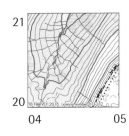

1:40,000 BMC/Harvey British
Mountain Map – Brecon Beacons

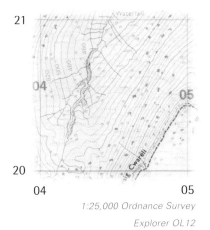

1:25,000 Ordnance Survey
Explorer OL12

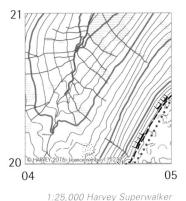

1:25,000 Harvey Superwalker
Brecon Beacons East

Figure 1 | Map extracts (to scale). OS extracts © Crown copyright 2016 OS 100057756. Harvey map extracts © Harvey Map Services Ltd 2016.

On the plus side, Ordnance Survey (OS) maps are well known, widely available, and cover the whole of the United Kingdom. They are available in a number of formats, two of which are suitable for our purposes – the Landranger series at a scale of 1:50,000, and the more detailed Explorer series at a scale of 1:25,000. The implications of different scales are discussed in Chapter 6.

Harvey maps are less well known, less widely available, and do not cover the whole of the United Kingdom, although they do cover most popular walking and mountain areas, particularly those in Scotland. Like the OS maps, they too are available in a number of formats, including British Mountain Maps at a scale of 1:40,000 (published in association with the British Mountaineering Council), and the larger scale Superwalker series at a scale of 1:25,000. Both types are printed on waterproof paper. Harvey also produce Ultramaps (a series of lightweight, waterproof 1:40,000 scale maps with a unique folding system), a series of route maps covering many of Britain's long distance footpaths and National Trails, and a number of large scale summit maps.

The main advantage of Harvey maps over OS maps is that they have been produced specifically for walkers and climbers, so things that do not appear on the ground (such as boundaries) are not shown. Additionally, the portrayal of rock features in complex areas is often clearer than on OS maps, with significant crags and even large boulders being marked with precision. The use of colour is also exceptionally good. For example, the density of woodland is indicated by the depth of green, the density of water is indicated by the depth of blue (marshy areas being indicated by a light blue shading), and in rocky areas, the colour of the contour lines changes from brown to grey (unlike OS maps, which use generic symbols that can obscure the contours).

One potential disadvantage is that Harvey maps use a contour interval of 15 metres whereas OS maps have a smaller contour interval of 10 metres in hilly terrain, and 5 metres in flatter terrain. In the most basic terms, the smaller the contour interval, the greater the amount of topographic detail that can be shown, which means that, in theory, OS maps can portray the general shape of the landscape in greater detail than Harvey maps. Whilst this is undoubt-edly true in subtler terrain as found, for example, in areas of gently undulating moorland, the larger contour interval on Harvey maps means they actually simplify complex terrain and show the outline shape of an area more clearly. Additionally, where particularly obvious land-scape features are missed because they lie between two contours, Harvey maps show an **auxiliary contour** to indicate the extent of the feature that would otherwise be missed (see also Chapter 8).

So which of these maps is best suited to our purposes? The truth of the matter is that they all are, for they all give similar information but in different ways! Assuming maps of identical scale, in really complex, rocky terrain, Harvey maps can be clearer and less cluttered than OS maps, whereas in more featureless terrain such as gently undulating moorland, OS maps can portray the landscape in greater detail than Harvey maps. Different people will prefer different mapping styles, so my advice is to gain as much experience as possible of using both

styles, and different scales. There is, for example, little point in using a 1:25,000 scale map in snow-covered terrain when many of the features shown on the map are obscured. In these conditions, a 1:40,000 (or even 1:50,000) scale map will be more than adequate.

Harvey maps are produced on waterproof paper whereas standard OS maps are not. Owing to the vagaries of the British weather, it makes sense to have some form of protection for your map, and there are several options. You could, for example, buy a good quality, waterproof map case. The better of these are made from soft, pliable plastic which is light and durable, rather than the cheaper, rigid, shiny types which tend to go brittle and crack after only a few uses. Whatever the make, the map case should be large enough to hold a double fold of a standard OS paper map. One advantage of map cases is that the map is always open and to hand, and this makes consulting it at regular intervals far easier. They can also be secured to your rucksack via a lanyard, which means you are less likely to lose your map, even in very windy conditions. However, map cases have the habit of blowing wildly in the wind, threatening either to strangle you or to hit you in the face. This is particularly true if you hang them around your neck – so secure them to your waist belt instead! Another disadvantage is that you will experience major problems if you need to refold the map in wet weather!

One alternative is to buy a ready-laminated map. Although the OS produce their own *Active* maps, there are several other makes available, each using a slightly different coating, and whilst they are all significantly more expensive than paper maps, they last significantly longer. One advantage of laminated maps is that they have a write on, wipe off surface, and if you use a **Chinagraph pencil** (a soft wax pencil available from good art shops), you can write even in torrential rain yet wipe off with a couple of strong strokes of your thumb. On the down side, laminated maps are heavier and bulkier than are their paper counterparts, and because they are not secured in a map case, there is a danger that they will be stuffed in a pocket and neglected, or even dropped. Unless you have a jacket with an easily accessible map pocket, the best way to carry a laminated map is to stuff it carefully and securely under the shoulder strap of your rucksack.

Another option is to buy a standard paper map and cut it into smaller sections, each of which can then be laminated. You can either do this yourself using clear self-adhesive film, or – perhaps better – you can use a laminator. If you do not have access to one of these machines, your local copy shop or print shop will almost certainly be able to help.

Increasingly popular is the use of mapping software (such as Memory-Map and Anquet) which allows you to print the relevant extracts whenever you need them, either laminating these as above, or printing them on specialist plastic paper. You can also, of course, download digital mapping directly onto a map-enabled GPS device, smart phone or tablet. Apps such as OS Maps and ViewRanger are increasingly popular, but you should always carry a paper version of the map as well. Electronic mapping should never be seen as a replacement for a paper map (see also Chapter 18).

There is no right or wrong choice here – it is all down to personal preference. Have a look at what other walkers are using and ask their opinion, experiment with map cases and different types of laminated maps, and use whatever you find most convenient.

Finally, this chapter would not be complete without at least a passing mention of panoramic maps. These are like aerial photographs taken at a low angle, so you can see the shape of the land in three dimensions. I am not suggesting that you should take these out and about, but if you use them in conjunction with a standard map of the same area, they are an excellent learning aid as they will enable you to start seeing the landscape via the contour patterns. They can also be helpful when planning walks. The same is true of mapping software that offers such things as 3D panoramic views and fly-through options.

To recap

There are many different types and styles of map. The most useful for mountain and moorland navigation are those produced by the Ordnance Survey and Harvey, at scales of 1:50,000 (OS Landranger), 1:40,000 (British Mountain Maps) and 1:25,000 (OS Explorer and Harvey Superwalker). All have advantages and disadvantages.

Whatever type of map you use, you will need to protect it from the weather in some way. This can be done either by using a waterproof map case, or by using a laminated map, either bought or self-laminated. This is less important with Harvey maps as they are printed on waterproof material, although many people still use these in conjunction with a map case in order to give added protection and security.

Please note, unless stated otherwise, the examples I have given in the text refer to OS rather than Harvey/BMC maps, for no other reason than because the former are currently more popular and generally more readily available, especially south of the Scottish border.

3 GRID REFERENCES

Describing position

I make no apology for introducing grid references at this early stage of the book. My reasoning is simple, you need to understand how to use grid references in order for me to illustrate the things I am describing by using the map extracts printed in this book.

In any event, grid references are useful (and sometimes essential) because they enable you to pinpoint the location of a feature or position for someone else's benefit, or even for your own future reference. To do this solely by describing a position would take a long time, and unless you wrote reams of notes, would often be only an approximation. However, by using a simple sequence of numbers (and sometimes letters as well) it is possible to locate any position in the UK, quickly, easily, and with great accuracy.

If you look at any OS or Harvey map, you will immediately notice that it is divided into squares of equal size by a series of horizontal and vertical lines. These are known as **grid lines**, and the squares (naturally enough) are called **grid squares**. These grid lines extend across the whole of the UK, thus dividing it into squares, and this system of squares is known as the **National Grid**. Each grid line has a number, and these numbers are printed not only around the edges of the map, but also on the grid lines themselves on each double fold of the map.

The grid lines shown on the types of map we are going to use are always exactly one kilometre apart **on the ground**, so each square formed by them covers a land area of exactly 1km², the size of the square **on the map** being dependent upon the scale of that map. This is illustrated quite clearly in Figure 1. Additionally, because north is always at the top of this type of map, the vertical grid lines run north-south, and the horizontal grid lines, west-east. This orientation will become extremely significant later in the book when we see how to use our compass to manoeuvre (or *set*) the map, and to calculate and follow bearings.

The method used to work out a grid reference is simplicity itself, so long as you follow a few basic rules. Luckily, these rules are printed in the key of all relevant OS and Harvey maps, so you can always check whether you are quoting the figures in the correct order until you become familiar with the procedure.

Let's assume that you wish to give the approximate location of a feature. If there is only one such feature within the grid square in which it lies, you can specify its location by giving the reference of that grid square. This is known as a **four-figure grid reference**, and locates the object to within an area of 1km². In order to calculate this four-figure reference, you should proceed as follows.

Referring to Figure 2, run your finger up (or down) the grid line which forms the *left* edge of the square in which the feature is situated, until you reach either the top (or bottom) of the map, or come across the line's two-digit reference number printed on it (e.g. 25). Make a note of this number. Now run your finger to the left or right along the grid line that forms the *base* of the square in which the feature is situated. This line will also have a two-digit reference number (e.g. 09). The grid reference for that particular square is the first number (25) followed by the second number (09). The four-figure grid reference of that square is therefore 2509. Remember that you must always use both digits of a grid line's reference number – you can never have a three-figure grid reference; indeed, all grid references must have an even number of figures.

When quoting any grid reference, you must always start with the figures printed on the vertical lines (known as **eastings**, because their reference numbers increase as you go east), and follow these with the figures printed on the horizontal lines (known as **northings**, because their reference numbers increase as you go north). There are several things you can use to help you remember the correct order, my favourite being that when you draw a capital letter L, no matter whether you are left handed, right handed, or cack-handed, you always draw the down stroke before the cross stroke. The letter L in this case stands for 'Location', and the letter itself encloses the square of the feature you are locating.

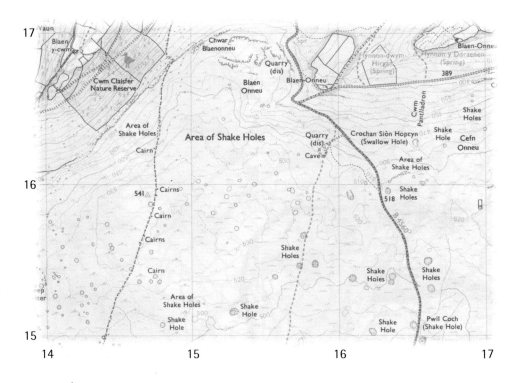

Map 1 | © Crown copyright 2016 OS 100057756.

Below are some examples of four-figure grid references of features shown on Map 1:

Trig Point 541 = 1415

Blaen Onneu = 1516

Crochan Sion Hopkin (Swallow Hole) = 1616

Grid references are universal. This means that the grid reference of a location taken from a 1:50,000 OS Landranger map will be exactly the same not only on the OS 1:25,000 Explorer map of the same area, but also the BMC 1:40,000 British Mountain Map, and the Harvey 1:25,000 Superwalker map. This is because all these maps use the National Grid.

A four-figure grid reference locates a feature to within a one kilometre square, which will usually be accurate enough, but there may be occasions when you need to be more precise.

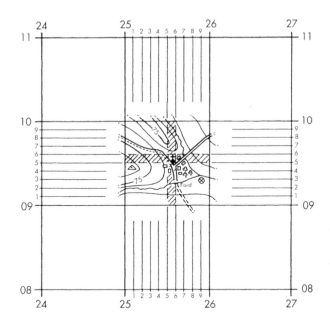

Figure 2 | Grid references. The grid reference of the church is 255095.

This is particularly true when, for example, there are two similar features in the same square. The standard way of doing this is by using a **six-figure grid reference**, which locates a feature to within a 100-metre square. This grid reference is calculated using exactly the same method as that of a four-figure grid reference, the first, second, fourth, and fifth figures referring to the grid square in which the object is located. Thus, a feature with a six-figure grid reference of 157165 will have a four-figure grid reference of 1516. This is simply another way of saying that it lies in grid square 1516. The third and sixth figures (in this example the 7 and the 5) locate the position of the feature within its grid square – the third figure (7) indicates that the feature lies seven tenths of a square to the *east* (right) of line 15; the sixth figure (5) indicates that it lies five tenths of a square to the *north* of (above) line 16. Thus, by giving the grid reference of the square in which a particular feature lies, and including in that reference an estimation of tenths of a square to the east (for the third figure) and the north (for the sixth figure), you can locate any feature to within 100 metres. Remember that the top of your map is always north, the bottom is south, the left edge, west, and the right edge, east.

The calculation of a six-figure grid reference is shown graphically in Figure 2. This also shows quite clearly that, contrary to popular belief, a grid reference refers to an area and *not* to a point. People who mistakenly believe grid references to be points often make mistakes when the feature they are locating lies close to one of the grid lines. If, for example, a feature lies slightly to the east of grid line 25 (neither exactly on it, nor more than one tenth of a square away from it), a common mistake is to give it a reference of 251***, simply because it is not lying on the grid line. In fact, the reference should be 250*** because it is situated less than a tenth of a grid square to the east of the line. This should be clear if you refer to Figure 2. All you have to remember when calculating the tenths, no matter whether you are calculating them from the north-south lines or the east-west lines, is that if a feature is less than a tenth away from the line the figure is 0. No matter where in the square, always round down the tenth.

You may think that I am being overly cautious here, but the difference in position between grid reference 123456 and grid reference 123457 can be as much as 99 metres – a significant difference if you are working in visibility of 50 metres or less, and particularly if you are using a GPS device which you have programmed using grid references!

Below are some examples of six-figure grid references of features shown on Map 1:

Trig point 541 = 147159
Road junction at Blaen Onneu = 157165
Crochan Sion Hopkin (Swallow Hole) = 165162

In some situations, and particularly when using a GPS compass (see Chapter 18), you may wish to be even more accurate. This can be done by giving an **eight-figure grid reference**, which locates a feature to within a 10 metre square. In order to do this with any accuracy, you need to be using a 1:25,000 scale map. The procedure is exactly the same as before except that you have to estimate hundredths of a square! Although this sounds like a tall order, it can actually be done fairly easily and surprisingly accurately by using a **romer scale** (see Chapter 6 and Figure 8). In the vast majority of situations, however, it is unnecessary to be this accurate, and most people will find that six-figure grid references are more than adequate. Indeed, if the feature you are locating only occurs once within its grid square, it is unnecessary to give even a six-figure grid reference – it will be sufficient to name the feature and give a four-figure grid reference (e.g. the trig point in grid square 1415).

If you are quoting the grid reference of a feature or position from some other part of the country, storing one for future reference, or sending the location of a rendezvous to a friend, it would be helpful if you also quoted the number or name of the map from which it was taken (e.g. Landranger 161, or Harvey Superwalker: Brecon Beacons East). To be absolutely correct, you should quote the **grid letters**, as shown in the map's key. This is because the grid line reference numbers run from 00 to 99 and then start again, so although any four-, six- or eight-figure grid reference is unique for the map from which it was taken, the same figures

will recur at intervals of 100 kilometres all over the country. To get around this problem, each 100 kilometre block of figures has two letters to distinguish it from its neighbours. Unless you are using a GPS compass, it is rarely necessary to quote the grid letters, but if you want a truly unique grid reference, you should place the grid letters in front of the figures (e.g. SO147159).

The ability to calculate accurate grid references is extremely useful as it will allow you, for example, to get locations from guide books or compare notes with other people quickly and with the minimum of effort. Accurate grid references of more than six figures are also essential if you wish to use a GPS device to maximum effect (see Chapter 18).

To recap

A grid reference is a way of locating any object, feature or position, anywhere in the country, with considerable accuracy. It is calculated according to a set procedure, using the grid lines printed on every map. You should always quote the reference figures of the vertical lines (eastings) before quoting those of the horizontal lines (northings).

All relevant OS and Harvey maps give an example of how to calculate a six-figure grid reference in their key. Until you are familiar and happy with the procedure, these examples enable you to check that you are quoting the figures in the correct order. With practice, you will find using grid references both quick and easy.

The ability to work out accurate grid references of six figures or more is essential if you are intending to use a GPS device to best effect.

4 MAP READING VS MAP INTERPRETATION

In the Introduction, I said that map work (and particularly map interpretation) should account for a good 90% of your navigation. Most people have a basic understanding of how to read a map, but when crossing difficult terrain in thick mist, map reading is not enough. You need to take it a stage further and develop the ability to interpret your map, and this skill can only be learned through practical experience. At the ultimate extreme, in severe, perhaps whiteout, conditions, when you are trying to find a bothy but are uncertain of your precise location, having the ability to interpret your map can literally make the difference between life and death.

Map interpretation is a two-way process – not only should you be able to tell the lie of the land from the map, but you should also be able to use the shape of the country around you to enable you to find your position accurately. It is the latter point, in particular, that will require practice.

Map reading is what you do when driving between Dartmoor and the Cairngorms. It is also all you need to do when walking on a reasonable path in good visibility. Map interpretation is what you do when walking on Dartmoor or the Cairngorms in poor visibility. There is a quantum difference between the two, and this can best be illustrated by the example of reading a book written in a foreign language. Someone with a small working knowledge of that language could, with difficulty, read the book, referring to a dictionary every now and then, and after a fair degree of effort, having missed many of the subtleties of description and characterisation, could glean a basic picture of the plot. Someone fluent in that language, however, would understand the book far better and more quickly, gaining a vastly more accurate picture of the plot, appreciating some of the subtler phrases, and having a better overall feel for the subject on first reading. If the book contains long or unusual words, even the most fluent person may have to refer to a dictionary on occasions. The person with the small working knowledge of the language can be likened to someone who reads the map, the dictionary being the equivalent of the map's key. The person more fluent in the language is the equivalent of someone who is able to interpret the map.

Map interpretation enables you to get an overall feel for the land as soon as you open the map, and it also allows you to appreciate the subtleties of landscape shape (via the contour lines) and other features (via map symbols or **conventional signs**). To put it more succinctly, a person who is good at map interpretation is able to see the landscape instead of seeing just a mass of colours, lines and symbols.

Photo 3 | *Map interpretation is about detail. It allows you to see not just the track, but also the fence to the right, the slope to the left and the ruin. It allows you to predict, in poor visibility, the route of the track and the shape of the land in the distance.*

One of the quickest ways to begin interpreting your map rather than just reading it is to imagine that it is constructed using a series of 'layers', as described in the next chapter. When you look at a map, you build up your picture of the ground, layer by layer, getting as much information as possible about each layer before moving on to the next. Although a simple technique, it does take a special type of visual discipline, and no matter how good your eyesight, you will find it helpful to use some form of magnifying lens.

I always carry two different types of magnifiers when on the hill. The first is the lens in the base plate of my compass. This is useful when trying to get as much detail as possible about small areas or pinpoint features. The second is a small, plastic sheet magnifier, available from good outdoor shops and commercial stationers. Although the magnification is not as powerful as that of the compass lens, sheet magnifiers are extremely useful in those situations where you want to get a better general impression of a larger area. For example, whilst it is sometimes difficult to see the pattern of contours in a heavily wooded or rocky area, because all the other symbols confuse the eye, a sheet magnifier will help you to see the pattern far more easily and with greater clarity. There is a definite technique. Place the sheet over the chosen area on the map, concentrate on the contours, and slowly lift the lens away from the map, 'lifting' the contours from the other layers as you do so. When done correctly for the first time, many people are amazed at just how much clearer the map becomes, and how much additional information they can obtain about the shape of the land.

To recap

Map interpretation is the most important skill there is in the art of mountain and moorland navigation. It requires visual discipline and concentration, but it will allow you to read the map like an encyclopaedia that gives you an incredibly detailed description of the ground. A surprisingly large number of people either do not realise just how much detail there is on a good map, or have difficulty in accessing it effectively.

Magnifying lenses are extremely useful aids to map interpretation. You should use two types – a fairly powerful lens such as is found in the base plate of a good compass (useful for looking a specific features), and a less powerful but slightly larger sheet magnifier (useful for getting a good general impression of terrain over a larger area).

5 CONVENTIONAL SIGNS

Using the layer system

Conventional signs are a form of shorthand used by cartographers to represent various features, both physical (roads, streams, buildings, etc.) and less physical (boundaries, spot heights, tourist information, etc.). The symbols are similar throughout both OS and Harvey maps, and are often either self-explanatory or fairly intuitive. In any case, a selection of the more common symbols is shown in the **key** of every map. Whilst it is unlikely that you will need to recognise all of these symbols, you should certainly try to learn the more common ones so that you can recognise them immediately without having constantly to refer to the key. For example, although you may not need to know the difference between the symbols for a church with a spire, a church with a tower and a church with neither, it would be helpful if you recognised that they all refer to a church, and it is obviously important that you know the symbols for features such as cliffs and steep slopes. It would also be useful if you are able to recognise which is the base and which is the top!

Before we go on to look at these conventional signs in more detail, we need to consider another important point – the age of your map. This is easy to check, as every OS and Harvey map has its latest revision date printed in the key. However, particularly with OS maps, you should be aware that 'revisions' often mean only major road improvements, or major industrial and residential developments, and that minor things like the odd new house or demolished barn will not be shown. Many of even the most modern OS maps of mountain areas are based on surveys done decades ago, but this usually presents few problems because little has changed. The fact of the matter is that all maps are effectively out of date before they are even printed, and it may well be that, since your map was produced, a farmer has demolished a fence, grubbed up a hedge or divided a large field into two. The possibilities are endless. A new housing estate may have been constructed in the valley, a road may have been improved by having its corners straightened, mature woods are felled, new woods are planted, footpaths become overgrown and disappear through lack of use, old cairns are removed and new ones built. As a consequence an awareness of the static nature of a map versus the dynamic nature of the landscape is of paramount importance, and needs to be borne in mind at all times.

Another important consideration is that the vast majority of surveying in areas away from roads is done using aerial or satellite survey, and not by a team of surveyors on the ground, although Harvey maps are often better in this respect than OS maps. What this means, in the most basic terms, is that if something can be seen from the air, it will be shown on the map – but you can see lots of things from the air that are totally invisible on the ground, ancient tracks and overgrown paths being common examples. Similarly, if it cannot be seen from the air, it may not be shown on the map – but there are plenty of features which are obvious on the ground but not from the air, such as low cairns in a rocky area, or surface streams on a bracken-covered slope. Although many people would agree that British maps are the best maps in the world, they do have limitations, and you need to be aware of these **limitations of mapping**.

Photo 4 | *In order to interpret your map, you need to look at it carefully, and in a structured way.*

In order to interpret your map effectively, you need to be able to access the relevant information, quickly and accurately, and preferably with as little mental effort as possible. Although arguably the best maps in the world, OS maps are not 100% user-friendly so far as walkers and climbers are concerned, simply because they are designed to be used by everyone and therefore show a whole host of information that is totally irrelevant for our purposes. Unfortunately, when we look at our map, it is usually the irrelevant information that we see first, and this has the effect of camouflaging the more important information which lies beneath.

No matter what type of map you are using, in order to get the most information from it in a usable form, you need to look at it in a disciplined and structured way. This is best done by dividing the conventional signs into a series of categories. In effect, what you are doing is thinking of the map as being constructed from a number of **layers**. To interpret your map, you look at each layer in turn in order to build up a highly accurate picture of the ground, stage by stage.

There are five categories of conventional signs – five layers of the map – which I am going to describe in order of increasing importance. The first layer includes symbols that are virtually useless for our purposes; the fifth layer comprises a single symbol without which everything else flies apart. Indeed, it is possible to navigate successfully using layer five alone.

The way you use the layer system is described in more detail in Chapter 8.

Layer one – 'symbols for things that aren't there!'

Let me give you a scenario – one which we will use throughout the book (and one which may already be familiar to some readers!). You are standing in the middle of a gently undulating expanse of heather moorland with only a rough idea of where you are. It is becoming increasingly misty – indeed, visibility is now less than 100 metres – and you have decided that the time has come for you to get a more accurate idea of your position. Looking at your approximate area on the map, you see that there is a small symbol. It is logical to think that if you can find the feature that the symbol represents, you will know where you are, but when you look for the symbol in the key of the map, you find that it indicates a 'site of battle'. Not very helpful!

You then notice that there is a long, black, dotted line that crosses the moor. This appears, on first glance, to be very useful, for if you head directly towards it, you are bound to hit it.

However, when you check this symbol in the key of the map, you discover it represents the line of a European Constituency boundary – possibly even less helpful than the battle site!

On OS maps, there is a whole host of symbols like this, ranging from European Constituency boundaries to sites of antiquity. Such things are not shown on Harvey maps. Even some of the labelling on the map can be considered in the same way. For example, particularly in more remote areas, large stretches of landscape can be effectively obscured by large black letters telling you the name of the area – something compounded in the Welsh hills by the fact that these names are often given in two languages! The lettering on Harvey maps tends to be smaller and more carefully placed, but still has the potential to obscure useful information.

Like any good rule, there are exceptions, and a couple of these 'symbols for things that aren't there' are very useful. The first of these is the **spot height**.

A spot height is simply a surveyed height above sea level. The easiest way to find one is to find a road on the map (any road will do) and run your finger along it. Within the distance of two or three grid squares you will see some black numbers, and if you look very closely (possibly using the lens on your compass), you will see that associated with these black numbers there is a tiny, black dot, usually (though not always) in the middle of the road. The numbers give the height of the dot, in metres, above sea level, and one reason spot heights are useful is that, by comparing two adjacent spot heights, you can begin to get an idea of the **aspect of slope**, or what is up and what is down. Aspect of slope (or which way a slope faces) is important for

Photo 5 | *It can be very difficult to pinpoint your location when standing in the middle of a stretch of moorland.*

several reasons. Not only is it helpful to know whether you are heading towards the top or bottom of a cliff, but having an appreciation of the aspect of slope is also essential when trying to see the shape of the land.

However, there is more to spot heights than initially meets the eye, for (on OS Explorer maps at least) there are actually two different types – black ones (such as the one on the road at 048266 on Map 2) and brown ones (such as the one on the hillside at 049262 on Map 2). You are more likely to find brown spot heights away from the roads – the figures will be written in bold brown and there will be a bold brown dot associated with them. Do not get confused between brown spot heights and the numbers written on the contour lines – the latter are written in less bold brown.

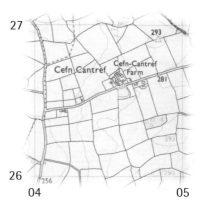

The difference between black and brown spot heights is simple but very important – black spot heights have been determined by ground survey (in other words, a team of surveyors has actually been to that spot and worked out the height), whereas brown spot heights have been determined by aerial survey (in other words, surveyors have not been to that spot). Brown spot heights therefore indicate something that is both visible and reasonably easily recognisable from the air, such as the ends of spurs, high points on ridges, and small or subsidiary summits, and these often make useful navigation features. Brown spot heights on Explorer maps and off-road black spot heights on Landranger maps are therefore as much **pinpoint symbols** (see layer 3) as they are 'symbols for things that aren't there'! Indeed, although there is nothing on the ground to indicate the location of either black or brown spot heights, if you think laterally, you can always work out their location – brown spot heights are always located on small landscape features; black spot heights are always at easily identifiable positions such as road junctions, the intersection of a road and a field boundary, or the brow of a hill. There are fewer spot heights shown on Harvey maps, and those that are shown have all been determined by aerial survey but are coloured black.

The second type of 'symbols for things that aren't there' that are useful are place names. Particularly in mountain and moorland areas, and in the larger or more remote rural regions, place names are often ancient and very descriptive. The problem is that they are also most usually in the original local language – in Wales they tend to be Celtic or Welsh, in Scotland they tend to be Gaelic, etc. If, for example, you know that (on Welsh maps) 'Carreg Goch' means 'red rock', or that 'Bwlch Mawr' means 'large col', then you have an extra piece of information that may be helpful when navigating. For this reason, a small glossary of local place names can be useful – such as can sometimes be found on tourist postcards.

Don't get me wrong; I am not suggesting you need to carry a Welsh or Gaelic dictionary, or that translating local place names is of vital importance (after all, we are still discussing the least important layer of the map), but I do believe that in order to navigate simply and successfully, you need to get as much information as possible about your surroundings, both from the ground and from the map.

Layer two – area symbols

Moving up slightly in order of importance, the second layer of conventional signs is **area symbols** – those symbols that indicate things like areas of water, areas of rock, different types of vegetation, etc.

These symbols are actually far more comprehensive than many people think. For example, on OS maps there are different symbols for coniferous woodland, deciduous woodland, mixed woodland, and coppice; for areas of scrub, bracken, heath and rough grassland (Explorer maps only); for outcrops, boulder fields, loose rock, and scree; for marsh, reeds and saltings. In coastal areas, different colours are used to differentiate between sand, mud and shingle. On Harvey maps, different colours are used to differentiate between open woodland and dense plantation, and between improved pasture, rough pasture, and fell or moorland, whilst different symbols (or colours) are used to denote boulder fields, scattered rocks and boulders, predominantly rocky ground, limestone pavement, peat hags, marshy ground, and sand or mud. As you can see, the list is quite comprehensive.

Photo 6 | *Area symbols can be less than helpful in situations such as this, but it would be different if you were standing on the edge of a boulder field or had recently crossed a bog.*

Going back to our moorland scenario, the fact that the map shows heath when you are standing in an area of gently undulating heather moorland is not going to be of much help, but it would be a different matter if you had recently come across a particularly boggy area, or were standing on the edge of a boulder field.

Whilst it is rarely possible to pinpoint your position using only these symbols, they are very useful in a number of ways. For example, they give you information which is helpful when you are trying to relocate – if you are surrounded by grassland you obviously cannot be in an area shown as being covered in boulders. In other words, area symbols can sometimes be used to narrow down your options – to show you 'where you are not'. They can also be helpful when route planning or route finding, as anyone who has tried to force their way through a coniferous plantation will tell you! Furthermore, they can be used to help you gauge your progress on a given route. For example, mountain walks sometimes start from car parks in valleys, where you begin by walking across enclosed farmland on footpaths to reach a stile over the hill fence, and then continue through an area of bracken before reaching the open heather-clad hillside above. All this – the enclosed farmland, the bracken, the heather and the open fell – is shown on Explorer maps, and Harvey maps use colour to differentiate between improved pasture, rough pasture, and fell or moorland.

On the flip side, and particularly when using those area symbols that denote different vegetation types, always bear in mind that such things can alter, not only from season to season, but also more permanently. Forestry, in particular, can change dramatically during the life of a map. If an area has been clear-felled or recently planted, it should be reasonably obvious, but let us suppose that you are using a map based on a survey done during the late 1990s, and that not long after the map was surveyed, an area of land was bought by a commercial forestry group and planted with sitka spruce – a tree that can grow by up to a metre each year. You are striding out, confident about where you are even though visibility is not fantastic, expecting to top a rise and descend into open countryside, when through the mist loom serried ranks of 10 metre-high trees! Let's be honest – your immediate reaction is not going to be, "Oh look, the map's wrong," is it? It is more likely to be, "What the…?" as your confidence drains away. There is a lot of psychology at work here.

Layer three – pinpoint symbols

The third layer comprises **pinpoint symbols**. These indicate features that are small or isolated, the classic example (in the British hills) being **triangulation pillars** or **trig points** (see Photo 7 and grid reference 217223 on Map 3) – the small concrete pillars commonly found at high points all over the country. Other examples include such things as pools, bothies, sheep shelters, and large cairns.

Pinpoint symbols are obviously more useful than area symbols. Indeed, many people believe that they are the most useful symbols of all, their reasoning being that if you can identify one on the map and can find it on the ground, you know exactly where you are. Whilst this is clearly indisputable, there are several other considerations, as detailed below.

Let's go back to our moorland scenario again. You have discounted the site of battle and the European Constituency boundary, and the fact that you are surrounded by heather is not particularly useful, but then you notice on the map that there is a trig point shown in your approximate area. On a clear day, this might be very helpful, but what are your chances of finding a small concrete pillar in a large tract of gently undulating moorland when the visibility is less than 50 metres? Unless you are starting from a known point and following an accurate compass bearing (or a path!), I suggest that finding it will be more a matter of luck than of judgement!

Let's take this a stage further. Imagine that you decide to look for the trig point, and a short distance later, you come across a small pool. If this is shown on the map, you now know where you are – or do you? What if there is more than one pool shown on the map? What if the pool is too small to be shown?

On a clear day, pinpoint symbols can be extremely useful, but navigating on a clear day is relatively straightforward because not only can you see your surroundings, but you can also usually identify potential hazards (such as the crag that is blocking your direct descent route) from afar. Additionally, because you can see so much, knowing your precise location is also less critical. In poor visibility, however, pinpoint symbols are only useful if you can positively identify them, and in order to do this with any reliability, you need to be aware of several important factors.

Firstly, when identifying symbols on the map and trying to find the corresponding feature on the ground, the very size of the feature is going to make it difficult to find – as in the example of the trig point given above. Additionally, thanks to satellite technology and the Global Positioning System, the Ordnance Survey no longer needs its trig points; some have actually disappeared having been removed by the landowner, so you might even be looking for a trig point that is no longer there. So too with other pinpoint symbols – can you be certain that the feature they refer to still exists? This is particularly true of

man-made features such as cairns – after all, man can make them but he can also take them! In any case, how do you tell one cairn from another, particularly in poor visibility? In my home area, for example, there are several cairns that are not shown on the map, and several that are shown but no longer exist! Indeed, cairns are probably the most notoriously unreliable features in mountain and moorland areas. The moral of the story is that it is perhaps unwise to use cairns as navigation points!

Secondly, having found a feature on the ground and you are trying to identify the corresponding symbol on the map, how can you be certain that it is the correct one? For example, one trig point looks very much like another. You may be on a mountain ridge, standing by a trig point, so you assume that you are at point 217223 on Map 3, whereas, in fact, you are standing at 207243! What if you are standing beside a small pool and there is more than one shown on the map? How can you tell them apart? Indeed, if the pool is small, it may not even be shown on your map. On Explorer maps, pools of less than about 10 metres in diameter are not shown, and the problem is far more significant if you are using a Landranger map, for pools of less than about 50 metres in diameter are rarely shown – yet in misty conditions, a 40 metre pool will seem enormous! Harvey maps are better in this respect, because if a pool is obvious on the ground, there is a good chance it will be shown on the map.

What I am trying to impress on you is that, by themselves, pinpoint symbols are not the most useful in terms of working out your position in poor visibility. However, when used in conjunction with other symbols, they can be invaluable. Additionally, once you have confirmed

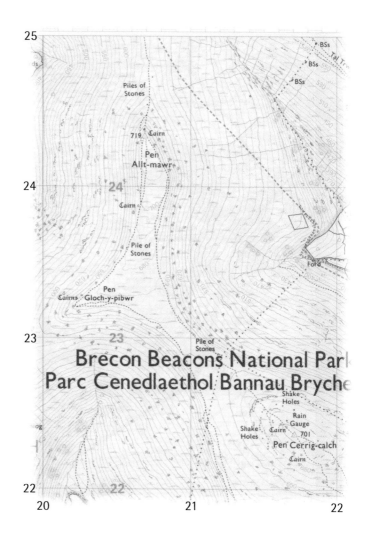

your position, pinpoint symbols are extremely useful as you can link them together using bearings (see Chapters 11 and 12), which enable you to walk from one known pinpoint feature to another in even the worst visibility.

It is the next two layers that are increasingly important and essential to successful navigation at any time, but particularly on those occasions when you find yourself staring at the inside of a cloud!

Layer four – linear features

The fourth layer of conventional signs comprises **linear features** – anything long and drawn-out, such as long field boundaries, paths, and roads. Natural landscape features such as streams, valleys, ridges and **breaks of slope** (see Figure 11) can also be used as linear features, as can the boundaries between two different types of vegetation (e.g. the edge of a forest).

The reason that linear features are so useful is simple – even when you do not know exactly where you are, if there is a long enough linear feature running roughly across your path and you head towards it, you are bound to hit it. Granted, you still do not know precisely where you are (except that you are somewhere along the feature), but you can then use the feature as a **handrail** and follow it to the left or to the right in order to reach a point where you *are* able to pinpoint your position. The best points to aim for are where two linear features cross. A classic example of this is descending from a mountain to reach a forest boundary, following the edge of the forest until you come to a stream, and working out your position at this point (see also Chapters 15 and 16). Similarly, and contrary to popular belief, there is nothing wrong with walking towards the top of a cliff in misty conditions, *so long as you realise it is there!* After all, it is a linear feature and you can use it to help with your navigation. The important exception is during winter conditions where you are not quite sure of your position and there is a danger of breaking through a cornice.

Particularly with linear features, some symbols are easy to misinterpret. It is, for example, of obvious importance that you can tell at a glance the difference between a boundary and a footpath (see grid square 2122 on Map 3) – many inexperienced (and not-so-inexperienced)

Photo 9 | *Linear features such as this fence are extremely useful, but always bear in mind that they can change.*

walkers have spent a futile half-hour searching for a footpath that never existed, all the time crossing and recrossing an invisible boundary. In situations such as this, unless you realise your mistake, you can easily think yourself lost when, in fact, you are not.

A common misinterpretation involves the field boundaries shown on OS Explorer and some Harvey maps. It is not unknown for people to interpret these black lines as dry stone walls, whereas they actually represent, as is said, the boundaries of fields. These boundaries can be anything the landowner wants them to be – walls, hedges, wooden or wire fences, even earth banks. In fact, there may be no physical feature to represent the boundary on the ground at all, the landowner having demolished it since the map was published. As has already been mentioned, it is important you bear in mind constantly that conventional signs give you information about features that were visible or that existed at the time the map was surveyed, and that things may well have changed since the map was published. What we need (and what we will get with the fifth layer) is something that is certain – something that cannot have changed however old or out of date the map.

Another common misconception concerns the meaning of the conventional sign for a **public right of way**. The presence of this symbol on the map does **not** mean that there is a well-defined footpath on the ground, although there may be – the symbol purely indicates that you have a legal right to walk there. Where this symbol and the symbol for a footpath (a black pecked or dashed line) are either superimposed or very close (grid square 1415 on Map 1), you will generally find some form of path (unless it has become overgrown through lack of use), but if the right of way symbol appears by itself (grid square 1515 on Map 1), you should be aware that there may not be any visible path. There are historical reasons for this confusion – indeed, many of the black pecked lines indicate paths that were visible from the air during surveys as long ago as the 1940s, whereas the public right of way symbols were not put on maps until after the introduction of the National Parks and Access to the Countryside Act 1949, and are updated at each map revision. Harvey maps, being designed and drawn specifically for walkers, are often clearer than OS maps in this respect.

In practice, when you are in enclosed farmland you should keep to the line of the right of way symbols, as these have been taken from Definitive Maps, which are legal documents supplied to the OS by the Highways Authority. When in more open countryside, and particularly when in **access land** created under the Countryside and Rights of Way Act 2000 (CRoW), you usually have the right to wander at will, although some local restrictions may apply. If you are visiting an area for the first time, you can get up-to-date access information online.

Some linear symbols are ambiguous by their very nature. For example, the symbol for a footpath is a pecked line (a series of dashes), but this symbol is also used to indicate other things, such as the edge of an unfenced road, or the boundary between two different types of vegetation. This means that if you see a solid black line with a pecked line running alongside (see grid square 1416 on Map 1 and grid reference 210166 on Map 5), you do not know (on first glance) whether this indicates a track that is fenced on one side and unfenced on the other, or a boundary with a footpath running alongside. In practice, this is rarely a problem as there are usually additional clues to aid your interpretation. However, the ambiguity remains a possibility and you need to bear such things in mind.

Whilst it is important that you realise your map can be wrong, and despite all these possible ambiguities and the fact that your brand-new map is out of date, you should always trust your map first and your judgement second. If you are ever in doubt about the accuracy of your map, ignore the lesser features (particularly the man-made ones), and try to concentrate on the shape of the land. It is, after all, the shape of the countryside (the topography) that is the most stable component, and things will not have changed radically, even if your map is based on a survey done decades ago. In Britain, we are lucky enough not to suffer from major earthquakes, and those factors that do have an affect on topography (such as landslip, quarrying and open-cast mining) tend to be obvious.

If you are going to work out the shape of an area accurately from your map, you must be able to interpret the fifth and by far the most important layer of conventional signs.

Layer five – contour lines

A map is obviously a flat piece of paper, but the countryside is rarely totally flat, and nowhere less so than in the areas in which you are likely to be walking. There will be mountains and valleys, ridges, spurs, cliffs, terraces and bays, all manner of depressions and hillocks, and an infinite variety of other ups and downs. Cartographers represent these vertical differences by the use of a very special and extremely important conventional sign known as a **contour line** (or simply contour for short). The definition of a contour line is 'a line which joins points of equal height'. Unfortunately, this definition doesn't actually help us very much! So let's look at this symbol in a little more detail.

Contours are the lines that form the swirling patterns on your map. They are coloured a light orangey brown on OS maps, and – depending on the nature of the terrain – either brown or grey on Harvey maps. It is extremely important that you understand them, and equally essential that you learn how to interpret the patterns made by them. This is, without doubt, the most complicated part of map interpretation, but it is also undoubtedly the most important, so if you can master this one idea then you are well on your way to being a successful and accurate navigator. With experience and practice, you will be able to look at the patterns made by the contours and 'see' all those features mentioned above – the mountains and valleys, ridges and spurs, etc. Moreover, you will also be able to see the exact shape of the slopes – where they are steep and where they are gentle, whether they are smooth or stepped, regular or irregular, and so on. When travelling along a path you will even be able to predict, well in advance, exactly what shape the land will be over the next horizon.

Each contour line on the map represents a particular height on the ground. Because each line joins points of equal height, every point lying along the same line will be at exactly the same height above sea level. The difference in height between the points on one contour line and the points on the next is known as the **vertical interval**, and this remains constant over the whole of the map. The vertical interval on all OS Landranger maps is 10 metres. It is also 10 metres on Explorer maps of mountain areas, but it can be 5 metres on Explorer maps of lowland areas, so it important that you check in the key. The contour interval on BMC Mountain Maps and Harvey Superwalker maps is 15 metres. The implications of these differing vertical intervals are discussed in Chapter 8.

Working on the basis that you are using an OS map of a mountainous area, all the points on any particular contour line are 10 metres below all the points on the contour line above it, and 10 metres above all the points on the contour line below it. We will discuss how you can tell which contour is above and which is below a little later. The basic concept of vertical interval is illustrated in Figure 3.

Despite the fact that many people start doing mental backward somersaults when it comes to interpreting contours, the basic idea is very straightforward. Indeed, you only need to understand one basic principle and be able to recognise three broad patterns in order to interpret any landscape, anywhere in the world! We will look at the three basic patterns shortly.

The basic principle is **the closer the lines are together; the steeper is the slope.** This is easily demonstrated. If, for example, the vertical interval is 10 metres, and there are five lines shown in a horizontal distance of one kilometre, it means that the land rises by 50 metres over that distance. If, however, there are 20 such lines in the same distance, it means that the land rises by 200 metres, and must therefore be that much steeper. For example, on Map 3 the ground in square 2022 is generally very steep, whereas the ground in 2122 is (for the most part) gently undulating.

One of the easiest ways to see how contours work is with a handful of coins. Place a fifty pence piece on a flat surface, then place a two pence piece centrally on top of it. Follow this with a ten pence piece, then a pound, a twenty pence piece, a penny and finally a five pence piece, in that order. If you now look at your pile of coins from the side, you will see – with a little imagination – that they form a conical, stepped 'hill'. If you now look at the coins from directly above, you will notice that the rims form a series of concentric circles. Each rim is a form of contour line that marks the height of each coin above the surface on which they are resting, and the thickness of each coin is its vertical interval. However, because each coin is of a different thickness

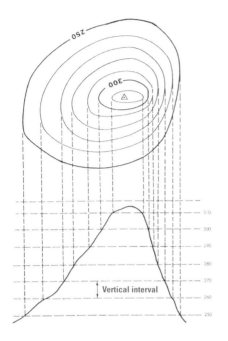

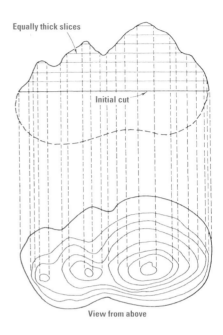

View from above

Figure 3 (left) | *Vertical interval. Note how the numbers always face uphill, and how every fifth line is darker. These darker lines are known as 'index contours'.*

Figure 4 (right) | *The potato hill!*

the vertical interval of the contour lines is not constant as it is on maps. Moreover, it is unlikely that you will ever find a hill shaped like a pile of coins. So let us now take it one stage further.

Find a large, oddly-shaped potato – the larger and more oddly-shaped, the better. Without peeling it, carefully cut it in half along one of its long axes and discard one of the halves. Now cut the remaining half into a number of equally thick slices, cutting along exactly the same plane as before. Place all these slices, in order, one on top of another, on a flat surface (see Figure 4). Looking at your half potato from one side, you will see – again, with a little imagination – what could be described as a strangely-shaped hill. Looking at it from directly above, you will see a number of lines, one between each slice. These lines are its contour lines, and the thickness of each slice is the vertical interval. On maps, contour lines represent the lines between equally thick imaginary slices of land.

By experimenting with your potato hill, carefully cutting out grooves to represent valleys, forming ridges and spurs etc., you will begin to see which patterns represent what shapes on the ground. You may like to have handy a map of an area that you know reasonably well so that you can compare your potato patterns with similar patterns on the map.

There are three basic patterns you should try to identify:

- A series of more or less parallel lines (the western half of grid squares 2024 and 2124 on Map 3). This pattern represents a more or less smooth slope, but you do not know which way the slope faces until you have worked out the aspect of slope (see below).

- A V or U shape (the western half of grid square 2022, or the south-western corner of grid square 2023, both on Map 3). This pattern represents a V or U shaped valley or spur, but, here again, you cannot tell whether it is a valley or a spur until you have worked out the aspect of slope.

- A series of more or less concentric circles (grid square 2122 on Map 3). This pattern represents a dome-shaped hill or a basin. Again, you need to work out the aspect of slope in order to find out which of the two possible features the shape represents.

It does not matter how big or small the basic shape, nor how many contour lines are involved; a U shaped pattern, for example, will *always* represent a U shaped valley or a rounded spur. Even if the U shape is formed by a single squiggle on a single contour line, it will represent a small U shaped valley or a small rounded spur. Indeed, one of the most useful contour patterns is a **ring contour** – a single contour which forms a small circle (grid reference 155162 on Map 1). Depending upon the aspect of slope, this indicates either a low hummock or a shallow basin.

Furthermore, the contour pattern mimics the shape of the landscape. Wide, swirling contours indicate a wide, swirling landscape whereas sharp, angular contours indicate a far more rugged terrain.

What should have become apparent by now is that certain landscape features, although totally different from one another, produce remarkably similar contour patterns. For example, there is little difference between the patterns representing valleys and those representing spurs, and a smooth slope going up to the left looks the same as a smooth slope going up to the right. In order to tell the difference between these similar patterns, you must be able to work out which way the slope faces. In navigation jargon, this is known as working out the **aspect of slope**, or which is the top and which is the bottom. Luckily, there are a number of simple ways in which this can be done.

In areas where space permits (where the contour lines are not too close together, or where there are few other significant surface features), some of the contour lines will be labelled with the height that they represent. These figures serve a dual purpose. Firstly, they tell you the height above sea level of all the points on that line. Secondly, by comparing adjacent figures you can easily work out the aspect of slope. If, for example, one line is labelled 550 and the next is labelled 560, you immediately know which way the slope faces. However, it is actually unnecessary for you to compare two or more figures because you can easily work out the aspect of slope from a single figure on a single contour line. This is because it is a convention in cartography that the figures are always written *the right way up* – in other words, the top of the figures always points uphill (see Figure 5). It is surprising how many experienced walkers do not realise this simple fact!

Figure 5 | *Contour labelling.*
Contour patterns are
ambiguous until you know
the 'aspect of slope'
(which way the slope
faces) as shown by the
numbers on the lines.

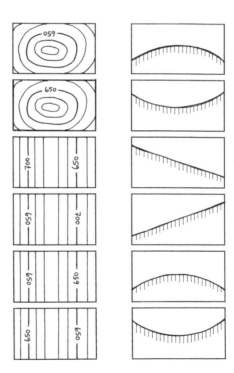

Another way in which you can work out the aspect of slope is by looking at the drainage of the area. After all, rivers don't flow uphill, neither are they usually found flowing along the tops of ridges or spurs! If you have a V or U shape with a river running along the centre, the chances are fairly good that it will be a valley – although there is bound to be somewhere in Britain with a river running down the centre of a spur, if only just to confuse us! In any event, it is usually reasonably easy to work out the direction of flow in upland areas, for most streams start at the heads of mountain valleys. If this is not immediately apparent, it is no great trial to trace the course of the stream until you find either its source, or its confluence with a larger river.

If you think about your map and the landscape it represents, you will understand that there are several other ways in which to work out the aspect of slope. For example, trig points usually occur at or near the high points of a particular area, so if you have a series of concentric circles with a trig point in the middle, the chances are good that the pattern represents a mountain rather than a basin. You could also compare two adjacent spot heights.

Because contour lines join points of equal height, the lines must theoretically be endless, appearing as misshaped circles. After all, you cannot have a point with no height, nor can you have a height that suddenly disappears. However, particularly in mountainous areas where the slopes can be very steep, you may find that the contour lines suddenly stop and are replaced by the conventional sign for a cliff or a steep slope. This is because, if the slopes are very steep, the contour lines will be so close together that it is impossible to distinguish between them. Indeed, if the cliff is vertical and of great height, the contour lines will be one on top of another. Happily, the conventional signs for cliffs and steep ground allow you to work out the aspect of slope because they distinguish between the top and bottom of the feature. They are therefore very important symbols. For example, if you use a magnifying lens to look at the difference between the representation of a cutting and an embankment, you will see that the symbol for steep slopes is actually made up from a series of small 'arrowheads', with the point of the arrow facing downhill (see Figure 6). With regard to cliffs, the symbol for a vertical face has a solid line representing the top (this is very clear on Harvey maps), but you should be careful that you have identified the right symbol because the conventional sign for outcrop on older OS maps can appear to be the other way around!

The area that people often find initially most difficult is relating the contour pattern to the landscape and vice versa. It will help if you try to understand the overall shape of the pattern before getting into the detail. Try to work out the basic shape first, and then start to clothe it in detail, using the layer system to help you build up your picture of the ground, piece by piece.

Once you are able to interpret the patterns made by a series of contour lines, you should start to appreciate the importance and meaning of otherwise insignificant little squiggles on single contour lines.

Some examples of contour line patterns and the shapes they represent are shown in Figure 7, and we will look at how you can best 'see' the landscape in more detail in Chapter 8.

Figure 6 | *The difference between a cutting (left) and an embankment (right), shown to illustrate the conventional sign for steep slopes.*

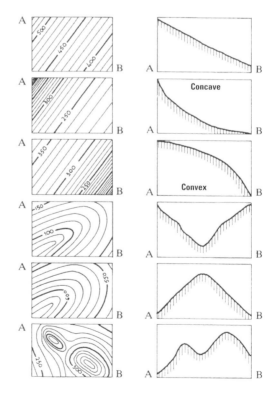

Figure 7 | *Contour patterns.*

To recap

Conventional signs are a form of shorthand used by cartographers to represent both obvious and not-so-obvious features on the ground. Since the map was published, some of these features may have been altered, or may even have disappeared altogether, and new features may have appeared that will not be shown on the map.

It helps to divide these conventional signs into five categories, these being:

- 'Symbols for things that aren't there'

- Area symbols

- Pinpoint symbols

- Linear features

- Contour lines

The most important of these are contour lines, and the patterns they create.

Contour lines are the conventional signs that cartographers use to indicate height. When used in conjunction with one another, they indicate the shape of the land. It is therefore very important that you understand them and are able to interpret the patterns made by them.

6 SCALE

Working out size and distance

The **scale** of the map you use is very important. Too small a scale, and the map will be unable to show the terrain in sufficient detail to be of any practical use in poor visibility. Too large a scale, and not only will the map show more detail than necessary, but you will also need to carry several sheets in order to cover the area that you might visit during a day's walk. Whilst there is no such thing as an ideal scale, maps of between 1:50,000 and 1:25,000 are the most common and practical. Maps of 1:63,360 (the old OS one inch to the mile series) are still around, but few people use them nowadays.

Scale is invariably stated as a ratio, which immediately alienates anyone who dislikes maths! Yet the concept is quite straightforward and the complicated looking figure is, in fact, very simple. For example, a scale of 1:50,000 simply means that one unit of length on the map (e.g. one centimetre) represents 50,000 of the same units of length on the ground (e.g. 50,000 centimetres, which is the same as 500 metres). This works for all scales, so at a scale of 1:25,000, one unit of measurement on the map is equal to 25,000 of the same units of measurement on the ground. The easiest way to remember what the ratio means is to change the : to = (e.g. 1 = 50,000).

Another helpful technique is to think of scale in terms of 'millimetres to metres'. First, when looking at the figures that tell you the scale, ignore all the figures after the comma (e.g. 25,000 becomes 25 and 50,000 becomes 50). Now think in terms of millimetres to metres – at a scale of 1:25,000, one millimetre on the map is equal to 25 metres on the ground, and at a scale of 1:50,000, one millimetre on the map is equal to 50 metres on the ground. It really is that simple!

Knowing what the scale means on the ground is all well and good, but it does not really help in a practical way because most people find it virtually impossible to visualise 25,000 of any-thing! Two things will help. First, because the grid lines on both OS and BMC/Harvey maps are always exactly one kilometre apart, this enables you to get a good idea of larger distances reasonably quickly, without having to measure them. Second, when looking at your map in more detail (as you will be doing when using map interpretation), it is much easier to deal with smaller numbers. Therefore, no matter what the scale of the map, use the 'millimetres to metres' rule outlined above. When, for example, using an Explorer or Harvey Superwalker map, both of which have a scale of 1:25,000, you will know that one millimetre on the map represents twenty-five metres on the ground. Twenty-five metres is a size that most people can visualise, especially if you can 'picture' the distance by relating it to a familiar object of a similar size. Different people use different things – leisure centre swimming pools are good (but not Olympic pools, which are 50 metres long), and I have colleagues who use 'just longer than a cricket pitch', 'about the size of a tennis court', 'a bit over the 25 yard line on a rugby pitch', 'the length of my back garden', etc. To make sure the technique works for you, try to find something familiar that you can visualise easily.

The scales used most commonly by walkers and climbers are 1:50,000 (OS Landranger), 1:40,000 (BMC British Mountain Maps) and 1:25,000 (OS Explorer and Harvey Superwalker). In terms of general usage, the 1:50,000 Landranger maps are slightly more popular, most likely because each map covers a greater area and therefore fewer maps are needed to cover a particular region. There are also historical reasons for this preference, because the original 1:25,000 scale maps each covered an area of only 100km², which meant that it was very easy to 'walk off the map' during a good day's walking! This made it necessary to take along a number of maps in order to cover the complete area to be walked, plus a little extra just in case you got lost and 'fell off the edges'! However, modern OS Explorer maps cover much larger areas and are becoming increasingly popular, and justifiably so, for they are undoubtedly far more helpful when extreme accuracy is needed.

The difference between **large-scale** and **small-scale** appears to cause some confusion. Perhaps the best way to explain this difference is to say that the larger the scale of the map, the more detail it will show. Because one needs space to show details, a large-scale map will cover a smaller area on the ground than a small-scale map of the same size (see Figure 1). On a 1:25,000 scale map, 1 millimetre on the map represents a distance of 25 metres on the ground, so 1 centimetre on the map represents a distance of 250 metres on the ground. A distance of 1 kilometre on the ground therefore takes up 4 centimetres on the map. On a 1:50,000 scale map, the same distance of 1 kilometre only takes up 2 centimetres on the map. Thus the smaller the number after the '1', the larger the scale of the map, and the greater the amount of detail that can be shown. For quick reference, the larger the scale, the larger the grid squares on the map, even though grid squares always cover an area of 1km² on the ground.

I am frequently asked which is the best scale to use. There is no simple answer. Whilst in many respects it is largely a matter of personal preference, a few things should be taken into consideration, as below:

- 1:50,000 scale maps cover a relatively large area and give a good general idea of the shape of the landscape, but they do not show as much detail as 1:25,000 scale maps. For example, there are no field boundaries on Landranger maps, neither are there any pools smaller than about 50 metres.

- 1:25,000 scale maps cover relatively smaller areas (one quarter the area of a similar sized 1:50,000 scale map), but are far more detailed. However, you should bear in mind the differences between OS Explorer maps and Harvey Superwalker maps, the main consideration being the difference in the vertical interval of the contour lines. The 10 metre contour interval used on OS maps in mountain areas (5 metres in flatter terrain) means that they can show subtleties in the shape of the land in greater detail than can the equivalent Harvey map, but whilst this is an advantage in some areas (particularly when you are wandering across gently undulating moorland), this detail can make map interpretation tricky in areas of complex, rocky terrain. Many people find that the 15 metre contour interval used on Harvey Superwalker maps allows them to interpret the outline shape in such complex areas more easily, and this is aided still further by the prominence given by Harvey cartographers to significant rock features, and by the use of **auxiliary contours**, which are used to indicate small but significant features that would otherwise be missed by the larger vertical interval (see also Chapter 8).

- 1:40,000 scale maps share some of the advantages (and disadvantages) of their larger and smaller scale brothers. The main advantages are that this scale is large enough to allow some detail to be shown (e.g. field boundaries and prominent rock features), yet small enough for the map to cover a reasonable area. On the down side, these maps are obviously not as detailed as the 1:25,000 scale maps, and some people find 1:40,000 an awkward scale when calculating distances (1mm = 40 metres). 1:40,000 scale maps also have a contour interval of 15 metres with all the attendant advantages and disadvantages.

I highly recommend that you gain experience of using maps of all scales, and until you can tell them apart at a glance, always check which scale you are using as there is a big difference between them. One of the quickest ways to judge the scale is to look at the size of the grid squares, but be aware that whilst the difference in size is obvious between 1:50,000 and 1:25,000 scales, it is less obvious between 1:50,000 and 1:40,000 scales (although, because Harvey and OS maps look completely different, the confusion should not occur). If you are familiar with Landranger maps and are trying Explorer or Superwalker maps for the first time, you will immediately notice a significant difference in the representation of distance, and the greater amount of detail shown. The difference between Landranger (1:50,000) and BMC British Mountain Maps (1:40,000) may be less marked, but it is no less significant. Whichever

Photo 12 | *1:25,000 scale maps give more detail than 1:50,000 scale maps, something that can be of particular use in relatively featureless moorland areas. Both the boulders and the depression are shown on the 1:25,000 scale map of this area; neither are shown on the 1:50,000 scale map.*

scale you use, always ensure that there is no possibility you might 'walk off the map', even if you miss your way. If your proposed route goes anywhere near the edge of the map, take along the adjoining sheet, just in case.

Once you know the scale of your map, you will be able to work out the size of features and the distances between them. This can be done quickly and approximately by referring to the grid lines, which are always exactly one kilometre apart, no matter what the scale. However, it is often useful (and sometimes essential) to calculate size and distance more accurately, and whilst it is a relatively simple matter to do this using a ruler (or the millimetre scale on the base plate of your compass) and then convert millimetres to metres, it is far easier to use a **romer scale**, as shown on the next page.

A romer scale is one which does the conversion from map distance to ground distance for you. Instead of reading off a map distance in millimetres and then converting this to metres, you simply read off the distance in metres. An added advantage is that you can use romer scales to measure very accurate grid references – an important consideration if you intend to use a GPS device.

All the compasses recommended later in this book have romer scales engraved into their base plates (see Chapter 10). If you already have a compass without such scales, you can buy separate romers covering all the common scales from most good gear shops. A typical separate romer scale is shown in Figure 8.

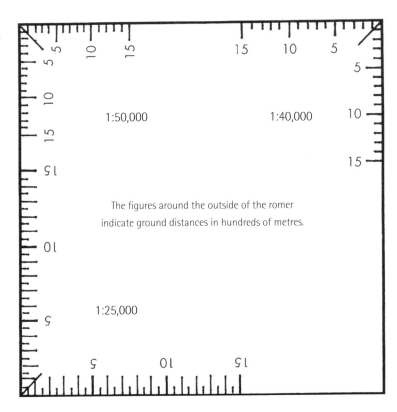

Figure 8 | Romer scale (to scale).

1:50,000

1:40,000

The figures around the outside of the romer
indicate ground distances in hundreds of metres.

1:25,000

To recap

Scale is simply the cartographer's way of indicating distance and size. A scale of 1:25,000 means
that one unit of length on the map represents 25,000 of the same units of length on the ground.
If you have any difficulty understanding the ratios, try changing the : to =.

No matter what scale you are using, it will help if you ignore the figures after the comma and think
in terms of 'millimetres to metres'. It is also useful to visualise familiar objects of known size as
an aid to judging size and distance.

You can get an approximate idea of distance on any map by referring to the grid lines, which are
always exactly one kilometre apart.

Measuring more precise distances from the map can be simplified by using a romer scale.

7 SETTING THE MAP

Holding the picture the right way up!

When you look at a picture, you usually try to hold it the right way up so that it makes sense! So, too, with a map.

A map is simply a picture of the ground, so in order to make the best sense of that picture, it is important that you hold it the right way up. This is known as **setting the map**, and it is one of the most useful yet least understood (and therefore least used) of all navigation techniques.

Many people new to map reading and interpretation hold their map so that they can read the writing – yet this is only correct when they are facing north. This is because all OS and BMC/ Harvey maps are drawn with the 'top' of the map facing north. So the top of the map is the northern edge of the picture, the bottom is the southern edge, the left side is the western edge, and the right side is the eastern edge. A correctly set map will always have its top (northern edge) pointing north.

So how do you set your map? In certain circumstances (when, for example, walking in poor visibility or crossing featureless terrain) it may be very difficult or even impossible to set your map without the aid of a compass. This technique is described below. However, it is often possible to set the map by eye, especially if your map interpretation is good. What is needed is some feature (or better still, a combination of features) that is obvious both on the ground and on the map. The best features of all are linear features such as paths, rivers, edges of forests, field boundaries, cliffs, ridges, spurs, and valleys – anything, in fact, which runs (more or less) in a straight line. All you need to do is turn the map in such a way that the feature shown on the map runs in exactly the same direction as the feature you see on the ground. Admittedly, you may find that you get a few attempts back-to-front (or 180° out), but this mistake should become quite apparent when you start to compare other features!

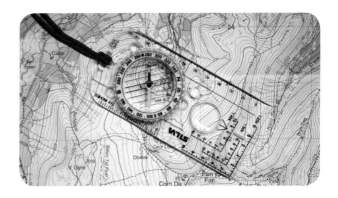

Where you cannot find any linear feature, you need to find a combination of at least two, preferably three, other features. For example, there may be a prominent mountain peak directly in front of you and a stream junction to your left. In this situation, you should turn your map so that the features on the ground appear in corresponding positions on the map – in other words, turn the map so that the mountain peak lies towards the part of the map furthest from you whilst the stream junction lies towards the left.

If you are unable to identify any features, or in situations where the visibility is too poor to see more than a few metres, you will need to use your compass. The easiest way to do this is to use the magnetic needle. Ignoring everything on the compass apart from the magnetic needle, place your compass on the map in such a way that the pivot of the needle lies close to a north-south grid line. Now **turn the map** (not the compass!) until the north-south grid lines run parallel to the needle, and the red (**north-seeking**) end of the needle points towards the top of the map. Your map is now set to within a few degrees (see Photo 13). For obvious reasons, you must ensure that you are using a north-south grid line rather than an east-west grid line, and that nothing metallic or magnetic is affecting the needle!

Whilst purists may argue that this technique is not 100% accurate (for reasons described in Chapter 11), it is sufficiently precise for the vast majority of situations in the UK for the next twenty years or so. If you are intending to use this technique abroad, or if you wish to be more precise, you will need to take into account an error factor known as **magnetic variation**. This is explained in Chapter 12.

With practice, this quick, simple and straightforward technique is suitable for use in the vast majority of situations. However, some people find it difficult to line up the needle and the grid lines with the required degree of accuracy. Additionally, if you are setting your map using

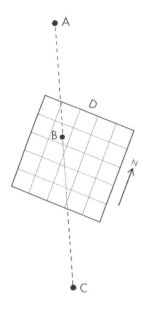

Figure 9 | *Single line of sight location with a set map.*
A = Feature on ground.
B = Feature on map.
C = Your viewpoint.
D = Top of map.

this method and then looking at features a long way off, the inherent inaccuracy will become magnified by the distance. In either of these situations, you will find it better to use one of the more accurate alternative techniques described in Chapter 12.

With your map set correctly, everything on the map is in exactly the same orientation as it is on the ground, and vice versa. This means that features behind you on the ground will be behind your position on the map, features to the left of your position on the map will be to the left of you on the ground, and so on. Setting the map therefore allows you to do some very useful things using **line of sight**. For example, let us assume that you are not sure of your position. Looking around, you see a feature to the left of you on the ground that you can recognise on the map. If you now set your map, you know that your position must be to the right of that feature on the map. Taking this one stage further, if you face the feature before setting your map and then imagine an invisible line that stretches from the feature on the ground, through the feature on the map, and back towards you, your position will be somewhere on that imaginary line between the feature on the map and you (see Figure 9). When using this technique, it helps if you hold the map horizontally in front of you, about level with your chin, and use some form of straight-edge (such as the base plate of your compass) to sight along and then to indicate the invisible line.

If you can see two features that you can identify on the map, you can be more precise in finding your position. First, face one of the features and set the map as described above. This time, instead of imagining the line and using a straight edge to indicate where the invisible line runs, physically draw it on your map (a laminated map and Chinagraph pencil will make life easier). Now face the other feature, check your map is still set, and do exactly the same, drawing a second line. Your position will be fairly close to where these two lines cross (see Figure 10). If you can see and identify more features, you can draw more lines and, theoretically, be more accurate. However, to

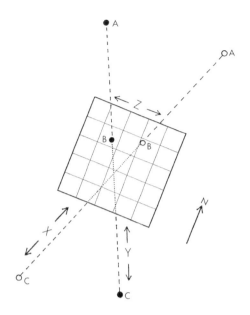

my way of thinking, if the visibility is good enough that it allows you to see two suitable features and get an approximate location, you should then be able to use map interpretation to get a more accurate fix. This technique is a simplified and practical version of a compass procedure called taking a **resection** – a technique which I believe to be less than useful in mountain and moorland scenarios, although it is discussed briefly in Chapter 15.

Let us now use a hypothetical example that illustrates another way in which setting the map can be useful. You have been enjoying your gently undulating section of heather moorland for some time when you notice a nasty-looking squall line rolling over the horizon towards you. Because you have been wandering more or less aimlessly, you do not have a very good idea of where you are, so you decide it might be prudent to work out a somewhat more accurate position before the visibility deteriorates. Once you know this, you will (as we will see later in this book) be able to navigate your way to wherever you wish, safely and with the least amount of difficulty, no matter how poor the visibility becomes.

Taking a good long look at your immediate surroundings, you notice a pool, only a short distance away, with a stream leading from it. Working out your position is always easier if you can identify a definite feature, so you move closer to the pool in the hope that you might be able to see one or more distinguishing features. You note from the map that there are

four pools in your approximate area, but one of them can be ruled out because it has no stream issuing from it, and another can be discounted because it is totally the wrong shape. This leaves you with two possible locations, and as they are some distance apart, you reason that it is important to identify which is which. You could take a compass bearing along the line of the stream (as described in Chapter 15) and then compare this with the direction of the two streams on the map, but there is an easier way! What you should do is set your map using, first, one pool, and then the other, each time lining up the stream on the map with the stream on the ground. Once the map is set, compare the topography with the contour patterns. You may find that when you line up the map using the first pool, the map shows the land sloping down to the left, whereas you can see that the land *rises* to the left. So you then line up the other pool and – hey presto! – the map shows the land rising to the left. Any other features that you can see are also in corresponding positions on the map. If you are still unsure and would like some form of confirmation, if you now put your compass on your map, you should find that the red end of the needle points north and the needle itself lies almost parallel to the north-south grid lines. Indeed, you could start by setting your map with your compass and then comparing the direction of the streams from both pools. Once you understand the rationale, the detail and how you use it is entirely up to you.

To recap

Setting the map is an extremely useful technique in which you turn your map so that everything on the map is in a corresponding or matching position on the ground. A correctly set map will have its northern edge pointing north.

Having your map set correctly enables you to navigate easily by using line of sight. It also allows you to work out your location by relating it to the position of known features that you can identify both on the ground and on the map.

8 SEEING THE LANDSCAPE

Building the picture in layers – map to ground

Map interpretation is a two-way process – not just working from map to ground, but also working from ground to map. Not only should you be able to use your map to work out the lie of the land, but you should also be able to use the shape and detail of the land around you in order to find your position on the map. So far, we have concentrated on accessing the information from the map. We now need to look at how we can process this information in such a way that we can start to 'see' the landscape, and how we can make best use of this information when out and about.

I am convinced that having the ability to interpret your map will actually enhance your walking pleasure. It will make you more aware of your surroundings, and will increase your appreciation of landscape. This is because, in order to use map interpretation efficiently, you need constantly to evaluate your surroundings, subconsciously storing any landscape information that might be useful. One thing that the best navigators have in common is that they are all very observant, with a keen awareness of their surroundings. In order to be truly observant, you have to use not only your eyes, but all your other senses as well. For example, if you are heading towards a stream junction in misty conditions, ask the people in your party to keep quiet every now and then, because you may well hear the stream long before you see it. Similarly, if you are heading towards a wood in poor visibility, you may well hear the wind in the leaves before you see the trees, or if it is a calm day in heavy mist, you may well smell the leaves! Many people can smell water, and most people can smell bog! Touch, too, can be useful. If, for example, you have been following a bearing with the wind on your left cheek and you notice that the wind is now coming from behind, does it mean that the wind has changed direction? Or have you made a mistake? It is certainly worth checking, but you need to be aware in order to notice the change. Good navigators become attuned to everything going on around them.

Photo 15 | *Having the ability to interpret your map will enhance your appreciation of landscape, allowing you to visualise not just the valley and the distant mountains, but the subtleties of shape, and even details such as the fence line.*

Whilst you need one type of observation to get information from the ground, you need a different type of observation – a special kind of visual discipline – to get the necessary information from the map. You need to study the map in such a way that you can select the right amount of information at the correct level of detail, and this will vary with the visibility and, to a lesser extent, the nature of the terrain. For example, let us assume that you are following a linear walk to a peak, and are intending to return along the same route. The outward journey is done in good visibility, and your landscape observation is such that when you pass a tiny V-shaped valley – a mere ripple on the landscape – you hardly notice it; it doesn't even register in your consciousness. Because you can see the surrounding landscape for a considerable distance, your map discipline is nearer map reading than map interpretation, and so you do not notice the tiny valley on the map – a V-shaped squiggle, just one millimetre across, reflected in two adjacent contour lines. On the return journey, however, the weather deteriorates and mist rolls in, and you soon find yourself in 20 metre visibility.

That tiny V-shaped squiggle on your map now becomes really important, for a 1 millimetre squiggle on a 1:25,000 scale map represents a feature that is 25 metres across! This means that the valley you hardly saw that morning is now a feature so large that you can hardly see the far side! Whilst I am not suggesting that you should be studying your map at this level of detail whenever you go walking, what I am trying to impress upon you is that there will be times when single squiggles on single contour lines become very significant, in which case you need to be looking at your map in sufficient detail to see them. It is in situations such as this where the 'layer system' becomes extremely helpful.

Let's start by working from the map to the ground. When looking at your map in order to see the landscape, you will find it easiest if you do so layer by layer, starting with layer five (the contour lines), and working your way towards layer one, thus building up your picture of the ground, layer by layer, piece by piece. Start by concentrating on the contours, and ignore everything else. This is difficult, but necessary! If you are in a complex area, it will help if you use a sheet magnifier and initially concentrate solely on the basic contour patterns. All you are trying to do at this stage is to work out the outline shape of the land. You need to do this in conjunction with the scale of the map in order to get some idea of size (remember, as a quick guide, the grid lines are always one kilometre apart). Once you have an idea of the outline shape, keep concentrating on the contours in order to put some detail into the landscape. For example, if you are looking at a slope, is it a smooth slope (in which case the contours are a uniform distance apart), a convex slope (in which the contours are closer together towards the bottom of the slope), or a concave slope (where the contours are closer together towards the top of the slope)? See Figure 7 for examples. Is there any obvious break of slope? This will be indicated where the contours are a set distance apart on one part of the slope, then a different distance apart on another part of the slope – see the central part of Map 4, Figure 11 and Photo 16. Are there any small spurs or valleys within the slope itself, or is it uniform (265347 on Map 4)? Are there any steps, terraces or platforms (268345 on Map 4)? Are there any ring contours (150151 on Map 1)? If so, do these represent hummocks or basins? The more detail you can pull from the map, the better – even if, at this stage, you cannot interpret exactly what landscape shape it represents.

Figure 11 | *Break of slope.*

 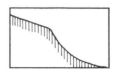

Once you have worked out the shape in as much detail as possible, start looking at layer four – the linear features. Some of these may be physical features indicated by the contour patterns – breaks of slope, ridge lines and valleys being the most obvious examples. Other physical features might include vertical faces and streams. Then there may be man-made features such as long field boundaries and paths. Remember, however, that you need to be careful with all man-made or vegetation features, as these may have disappeared since the map was surveyed, or they may no longer be obvious on the ground.

Once you have exhausted the linear features, look at layer three (the pinpoint symbols). Get into the habit of using a magnifying lens, not only to ensure that you get as much information as possible from the map, but also to confirm that you really are seeing what you think you see. When you are sure you have seen all the pinpoint symbols, look at layer two (the area symbols) in order to clothe the area in rocks or vegetation; then glance at layer one (the 'symbols for things that aren't there') in case there is anything else that helps. By building up your picture of the ground in this way, layer by layer, and in a structured manner, you are less likely to be overwhelmed by the amount of information shown on the map. It also means you are less likely to 'cherry pick' the information, which leads to the risk that you will miss subtleties that may be extremely useful.

PRACTICAL EXERCISE (SEE APPENDIX FOR ANSWERS)

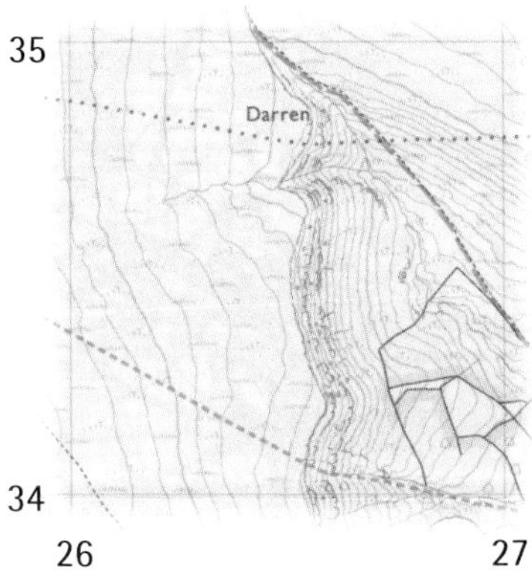

Map 4 | © Crown copyright 2016 OS 100057756.

Many people trying to interpret their map for the first time do not take the process far enough – they get the basic shape of the land, but fail to work out the detail. So let's illustrate the process with a practical example using Map 4. Imagine that you are hovering high above this grid square, looking down at the ground, and work out what you would see. Take some time to do this. Try to get as much detail as you can from the map so that you can picture the landscape, and when you believe you have got all the information possible, turn to the back of this book to see how well you did (and please let me know if you see anything that I have not mentioned!).

Building the picture in layers – ground to map

You also need to be able to do this process the other way round – working from the ground to the map. Indeed, it is preferable whenever possible to work in this way because it helps you to avoid the temptation to 'make things fit'. For example, if you are looking at your map in misty conditions, trying to relate the mass of information you can see on the map to the little that you can see on the ground, it is easy to imagine that the small amount that you can see fits with the map. If you do it the other way around, getting a small amount of information from the ground and then trying to fit this onto the map, you are far less likely to make a mistake.

The procedure to follow when working from ground to map is exactly the same as before – you should build up your picture of the ground (your 'mental map', if you like), layer by layer, starting with the shape of the land. Start macroscopically – ask yourself what is the basic shape of the land around you, and only then start to clothe it with detail. Although the precise procedure will be discussed in more detail in Chapter 25, there are a few things worth considering at this stage, simply because they will help you interpret your map more easily and accurately.

Photo 16 | *You can locate yourself fairly accurately anywhere on this plateau using the breaks of slope combined with the aspect of slope!*

First, when trying to see the contours in the landscape, it is helpful to imagine that the land is being inundated with flood water. Imagine the water lapping at your feet, and then try to visualise where the shoreline would be. This shoreline corresponds to the contour line at the height you are standing. Now imagine the floodwater either rising or falling by the same amount as the vertical interval of the contours on your map (10 metres on OS maps in mountain areas, and 15 metres on BMC/Harvey maps), and then try to visualise where the new shoreline would be. By imagining the landscape being flooded to different levels and then visualising where the shorelines would be, you will start to get a fairly good impression of the contour patterns in that area.

Second, you need to be aware of the implications of different vertical intervals. Mean sea level (0 metres) is taken from the Newlyn Tide Gauge which is located just south of Penzance on the south coast of Cornwall. For those of you interested, the tide gauge is located at grid reference SW467286 which is on OS Explorer 102 or OS Landranger 203. As we have already seen, Ordnance Survey maps in mountain areas have a vertical interval of 10 metres, so there is a new contour every 10 metres. Ten metres is actually quite big – about the size of a large house. What this means is that you can have a landscape feature slightly smaller than a house (say eight metres high) that starts at 411 metres above sea level and finishes at 419 metres above sea level, and it will *not* be visible on the map simply because it will not be reflected in the shape of any contour. However, conversely, you can have a landscape feature slightly smaller than a bungalow (say four metres high) that starts at 409 metres above sea level and finishes at 413 metres above sea level, and it *will* be visible on the map because it is reflected in the shape of the 410 metre contour. This is shown graphically in Figure 12. This single fact explains

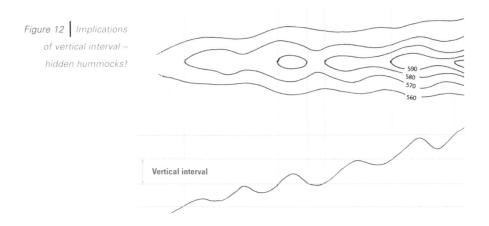

Figure 12 | *Implications of vertical interval – hidden hummocks!*

590
580
570
560

Vertical interval

why it is sometimes difficult to interpret the contours in gently undulating terrain such as that found in moorland areas. It also explains why OS maps, with their 10 metre vertical interval, are able to show the shape of subtle terrain in more detail than Harvey maps, which have a 15 metre vertical interval. Having said this, it is only fair to point out that Harvey's cartographers go a long way towards getting round this by using auxiliary contours to pick up significant features (often small hummocks) which would otherwise be missed because they lie between the 15 metre contour lines. These auxiliary contours have no set vertical interval, and although there is an inherent assumption that they will be at about 7.5 metres, this is not always the case.

Third, if you fully understand the principle of contour lines, you should be able to appreciate the concept that it is possible to climb and descend for up to 9.99 metres (OS) or 14.99 metres (Harvey) without crossing a contour line. To take a simple example, let us suppose that you are traversing a slope – in effect, you are walking between two contour lines. Because the land slopes between the two contours, the closer you get to the uphill contour, the higher you will be, and the closer you get to the downhill contour, the lower you will be. As a practical example, look at Map 5, and assume you are walking along the lane from east to west. Leaving Wenllan (217165), the lane immediately crosses the 150 metre contour and climbs 11 metres (crossing the 160 metre contour) to spot height 161. It then swings north and heads towards a sharp left-hand bend, descending 9 metres as it does so, getting closer to (but never crossing) the 150 metre contour. Swinging west again, it climbs slightly past Hen Castell (212165) (you know it must climb because it is getting closer to the 160 metre contour again), then swings right and descends towards the 150 metre contour, and then swings left again. Here, even though the lane is straight, it climbs slightly because the 160 metre contour curves towards it (211166). It then trends to the right and starts to descend, eventually crossing the 150 metre contour and dropping steeply past a small, tight U-shaped valley (208167) and reaching a junction.

Map 5 | © Crown copyright 2016 OS 100057756.

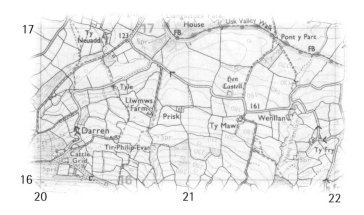

To give another, perhaps more practical example, look at Figure 13. If you really understand the concept you will recognise that if you walk in an easterly direction (from left to right) along the centre of the ridge, even though you are not crossing any contours, you will descend twice, reaching low points at point A and point C, and a high point at point B. The clue that tells you this is the way in which the 600 metre contours to either side pinch together, meaning that your route takes you closer to them.

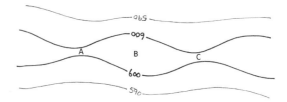

Figure 13 | *Predicting undulations along an apparently level ridge.*

Some people may ask, "So what?", thinking that I am being unnecessarily detailed – but to my mind, successful navigation is all about detail. Indeed, I believe that this concept is particularly important if you use BMC or Harvey maps, because on these it is possible for you to climb or descend for up to 15 metres without crossing a contour. In thick mist, a vertical distance of 15 metres can (and will) seem huge, and the danger is that you will assume you have crossed contours when, in fact, you have not – an assumption that could cause real problems when trying to work out your position. Awareness is an important key when unlocking the information on a map.

So how does map interpretation and picturing the ground help you when you are unsure of your location, and how can it be used effectively? Perhaps the best way to illustrate this is by giving some practical examples.

In the first example, you are standing on the slopes of a known mountain, but unsure of your precise location. Obviously, it is always helpful if there are a few definite or recognisable features nearby, so for this first example let us assume that you have no idea where you are on this mountain apart from the fact that you are standing at the junction of two streams. Straight away, things are not as bad as they could be – at least you know which mountain you're on, and you have a definite point of reference (the stream junction) from which to start working out your position.

Consulting your map, you are dismayed see that there are several stream junctions shown on the part of the mountain where you believe you are standing, and you realise that you could be at any of them. It is at this stage that map reading becomes ineffective – what is needed is map interpretation. Exactly what you do now will depend very much upon the situation at the time – there are no textbook answers because each situation you face will be totally different. For example, in this situation you could: (a) look at each stream junction on the map in more detail, (b) set your map in order to see if you can make the features on the ground correspond with the symbols on the map, or (c) look at the shape of the land around you, trying to fit this shape to the stream junctions shown on the map. In practice, in all but the most extreme situations, you will probably use a combination of all these techniques, and more. As it happens, this time you are lucky, because there is a substantial crag on the spur lying above the stream junction, and you see from the map that there is only one stream junction that is situated below a spur where there is a crag. You must, therefore, be standing at that stream junction.

I freely admit that this is a very simple example, but it does serve to illustrate a couple of important points. Firstly, I strongly doubt if you will ever be so lost that you have not got at least an approximate idea of your position – after all, you are not truly *lost* if you know which mountain you are on, although you may well feel 'locationally challenged'! Secondly, it is far easier to work out your position when you are standing at (or near) some form of identifiable feature than it is if you are standing in the middle of nowhere. Indeed, if you find yourself in the latter situation, it is often easier to carry on walking until you reach a definite feature, than it is to try and locate yourself solely by comparing the shape of the land around you with the contours on the map, and this is nowhere truer than when crossing moorland areas and bare mountain slopes. We will look at ways of recovering from this type of situation in Part Four. Obviously, you should be very wary of walking in poor visibility in areas where there are potential hazards such as large drops, and particularly in winter conditions where there may be cornices around.

In the second example, you are just about to descend into a valley after a good day's walking in an area that you have not visited before. As you begin the descent and the view of the valley unfolds, you are horrified to see a large block of forestry. Your immediate thought is that you are descending into the wrong valley because your map gives no indication of any woodland near your chosen route. Although you realise that this could be due to the fact that your map is out of date, not only do you know that you have the latest map, but you also see from the map that there is another valley nearby which has a patch of forestry in an equivalent position. What you have to decide is whether you are descending into the correct valley that has been afforested

Photo 17 | *It is extremely difficult to pinpoint your position unless you are standing by a definite feature!*

since your map was printed, or whether you are descending into the wrong valley, shown to be afforested on your map. It may well be that a single bearing (as described in Chapter 15) will solve the problem, but if your map interpretation is reasonable, you should be able to work things out simply by setting the map and comparing the topography with the contour patterns.

Owing to the fact that no two areas of land are precisely the same, it is impossible to give hard and fast rules relating to the way you solve these types of problems. At this level, navigation is very much an art rather than a science, and personal preference will have a significant role. Different people will solve similar problems in totally different ways, even though their preferred methods will all be based upon similar techniques. This is another reason, as emphasised in the introduction, that knowledge of the basic techniques is not enough – you must gain practical experience and become familiar with the techniques so that you are able to apply a certain amount of reasoning to the problems with which you are likely to be faced.

When you are able to set and interpret your map efficiently, you will find that you are able to predict what lies ahead of you. This is the start of accurate and successful navigation. You know the scale of your map (you have a quick reference via the grid lines), and by using this in conjunction with the different layers of conventional signs, especially the contour lines, you will find it increasingly easy to keep yourself on route. You may, for example, note from your map that in approximately 500 metres you will pass a small lake to your left and then start to go uphill. If, after 500 metres, you pass a small lake to your right and start to go downhill, you will know either that you are off route, or that your map work needs improvement. If, after a kilometre, you have seen no sign of any lake even though the visibility is excellent, I would respectfully suggest that you should turn around and retrace your steps back to the start!

In the remainder of this book, you will learn how to work out how many minutes it will take you to get to the lake, how many paces you will take on the way, and how you can get safely back to civilisation when the mist is so thick that you are unable to see the lake until you walk into it. Before you progress any further, however, you must master the art of map interpretation. All the techniques described later in this book rely on your ability to interpret a map, and are therefore virtually useless unless you can do so. Even if, at this stage, you find it difficult, if you persevere you will eventually start to see your map as a picture of the landscape rather than a mass of lines, symbols and colours.

To recap

Map interpretation is a two-way process – you should be able to use your map to work out the lie of the land, and you should also be able to use the shape and detail of the land in order to find your position on the map. Getting the information from the map requires a special kind of visual discipline. Getting the information from the ground requires excellent observation skills.

When working from map to ground, the easiest way to picture the landscape is by using the layer system as described in Chapter 5 – building up your picture layer by layer. The same applies when working from ground to map. The most important layer is the contour patterns. Always start by getting the basic shape, only then starting to clothe it with detail. In this way, you run less risk of 'cherry-picking' what you assume is the most important information, and of suffering 'information overload'!

When trying to work out the shapes indicated by the contour patterns, it is helpful to imagine that the land is becoming inundated with flood water, each successive shoreline representing a contour.

It is important that you recognise the implications of different vertical intervals, and understand the idea that it is possible to gain (or lose) a certain amount of height without having to cross a contour line.

PART 2 – THE COMPASS

So far, we have concentrated on map work in order to lay a firm foundation for the growth of your skill at navigation, for success and accuracy will always be based upon sound map interpretation. However, you will doubtless come across situations in which map interpretation does not suffice, and in these cases you will need some additional skills. The most important of these involve using a compass.

In this part of the book, we are going to look at various types of compass, and discuss basic compass bearings. Once you have become familiar with the basic principles, you will soon come to understand that the use of the compass is limited solely by your imagination. I have described some of the more creative compass techniques in Part Three, along with a variety of other skills that can be used as aids (*not* alternatives) to map interpretation, especially in poor visibility.

9 COPING WITH POOR VISIBILITY

When the weather conditions are fine and you have good visibility, finding your way around is usually relatively straightforward, and mistakes are rarely costly. You can see where you are going and where you have been, and you can usually get sufficient information from your surroundings to keep you (more or less) on course. In an area that is new to you, you may have to glance at your map occasionally to get a feel for the lie of the land, and in particularly featureless terrain you may have to glance at your compass every now and then in order to keep your sense of direction, but as long as you keep reasonably alert and focused, you will generally find few problems in getting around safely.

It is when the visibility deteriorates or things go wrong that navigation becomes more difficult, and the last thing you need is an unwieldy set of complicated procedures. The simpler the techniques, the more likely you are to use them, and the greater the chance that you will use them successfully. The potential for problems is compounded by the fact that your mind may well be full of other things. For example, you may be worried about the deteriorating weather conditions (visibility is now down to less than 50 metres) and the increasingly strong

Photo 18 | *Navigating in poor visibility – an exercise in damage limitation.*

wind (gusts of which have already blown you over a couple of times), about your companion (who is normally loud and extrovert but has been quiet and withdrawn for the past half hour), about the fact that it is nearly dusk and you are not sure of your exact position (except you know you are still a considerable way from your car), all coupled with concern about your ankle (which is increasingly painful as a result of an earlier stumble). In circumstances such as these, you are not going to want to perform complicated mathematical calculations in order to navigate to safety.

The good news is that you do not have to! I am going to boil everything down into simple, straightforward techniques that can be used anytime by anyone. Having said this, in the same way that map interpretation demands a degree of visual discipline, accurate poor visibility navigation (and compass work in particular) also demands discipline and focus.

Navigating in poor visibility can be likened to an exercise in damage limitation – the further you go on any single leg of navigation, the greater will be the potential error. In order to compensate for this, you should always work according to the **KISS principle**. This is very straightforward – Keep It Short and Simple. The shorter the distance between the point where you are and the point for which you are aiming, the smaller will be any compound error and the more likely you will be to find it. The simpler the procedures you use in order to reach that point (or to work out your current position), the more likely you are to use them, and the more chance you have of being successful. We will look at the KISS principle in more detail in Chapter 22.

To recap

Although map interpretation is the most important part of navigation, there will be times when you need a few additional techniques, the most important of which involve using a compass.

When you find yourself in poor visibility and deteriorating weather conditions, your mind will often be full of concern for things other than navigation, so it makes sense to use simple, straightforward techniques that do not require much brainpower! Additionally, poor visibility navigation is an exercise in damage limitation – the further you go between known points, the greater will be the potential error. Everything you do should therefore be based on the KISS principle – Keep It Short and Simple.

10 TYPES OF COMPASS

In its most basic form, a compass is simply a device that indicates direction. However, as we will see, a compass suitable for mountain and moorland navigation should be able to do far more than simply show you in which direction north lies! The problem facing the novice navigator is that compasses come in a huge variety of different shapes and sizes, some of which have been designed for specialist applications and are not particularly suited to our needs. This range extends from the old fashioned 'Boy Scout' or 'button' compasses, through incredibly expensive and heavy prismatic instruments that can be read to within a quarter of a degree, to modern electronic compasses and GPS devices. All types do the job for which they were designed, but many are of limited use when trying to navigate in misty conditions or across featureless terrain. Outline descriptions of the basic types are given below.

Button and pocket compasses

Button and pocket compasses are useful for getting a rough idea of direction, but little else. The better models have a swivel dial as opposed to a simple needle, and are liquid-filled in order to dampen the movement of the dial, which makes them easier to read. Although these compasses are unsuitable for micro-navigation (simply because they do not allow you to gauge your direction with sufficient accuracy), they are so small and light that you can pop one into the pocket of your rucksack in case something happens to your main compass. I keep one in my first aid kit.

Protractor compasses

Without doubt, by far the best and most commonly used compasses for mountain and moor-land navigation are **protractor compasses** (also known as **orienteering compasses, map compasses,** and **base plate compasses**). These actually consist of two separate parts: the compass housing (which contains the magnetic needle), and the base plate (which should contain a magnifying lens and one or more scales). In order that you can easily understand the compass techniques described later in this book, it will be helpful for you to get to know your way around the compass, as described below.

Referring to Figure 14, the **compass housing** [1] is a circular capsule inside which pivots the magnetic needle [2], one half of which is red, the other half being white. The red end of this needle is referred to as the **north-seeking end**, for it will try to point directly towards magnetic north – assuming, of course, that you are using your compass correctly, as described later! On some compasses, particularly optical sighting models (see below), the needle is replaced by a rotating disc or swivel dial, which has north and south (and sometimes east and west) clearly marked. The housing itself is filled with a clear liquid (usually alcohol or oil), which dampens the movement of the needle and thus makes the compass easier to read.

The rim of the compass housing is divided into 180 segments, each segment representing 2° of arc, and to help you when you are using bearings, some of these segments are numbered (usually at intervals of 20°) The **cardinal points** (north, south, east and west) are also marked in their relative positions. All this talk of degrees may be off-putting for those of you who, like me, dislike maths, but you do not have to be a whiz kid at geometry or trigonometry to be good at navigation. Having said this, it does help if you know that there are 360° in a circle, and that east is 90°, south is 180°, and west is 270°. North is both 0° and 360°. When buying a compass (for civilian use), make sure you get one that is calibrated in degrees rather than mils – this latter measurement is used for military purposes.

The transparent base of the compass housing is engraved with a number of fine, parallel lines (the **orienting lines** [3]), and the two central orienting lines are joined together to form an arrow (the **orienting arrow** [4]), which points to the same position as north on the rim of the housing. On the better modern compasses, the northern half of the orienting lines are coloured red, whilst the southern half are coloured black. This is done for two reasons: firstly, it helps you avoid one of the most common mistakes in compass navigation, being 180° out, (see Chapter 11); secondly, it helps you use a technique called **boxing** (see Chapter 15).

The way in which the compass housing is attached to the rest of the compass is extremely important, for any excessive movement will lead to inaccuracy. You should not, for example, be able to move the housing from side to side within its mounting, nor from front to back. In almost every model of compass, the housing is surrounded by a collar that fits snugly into the base plate in such a way that it can be turned through 360°. This movement should be smooth but reasonably firm. If it is too stiff, it will be difficult for you to set bearings accurately. Conversely, if it is too loose and the housing turns too freely, there is a danger that you may inadvertently alter the setting as you are following your bearing. This should be avoided at all costs, as it is one of the hardest mistakes to correct. With some models of compass, the housing is attached permanently to the base plate, whereas with others it can be removed.

The rectangular **base plate** [5] should be at least 10 centimetres long and 5.5 centimetres wide (12.5 centimetres x 6 centimetres is even better). Compasses with smaller base plates are widely available, but these lack the versatility afforded by the larger sizes. Whatever size base plate you choose, it should contain a magnifying lens [6] to aid map interpretation, and should also have one or more scales printed along the front and/or the sides [7]. Although these scales are commonly in centimetres and millimetres, the better models of compass have a very useful extra set of scales called romer scales (see also Chapter 6). This is particularly true of those models with larger base plates.

The base plate should have a number of fine, parallel lines engraved along its length, these lines being parallel to the sides. In most models, the central one of these lines has a large arrow at its front end [8] – this is known as the **direction of travel arrow**, commonly referred to as the **DOT arrow**. This same central line also runs back and intersects the compass housing where it is visible under the numbered segments [9]. This position on the compass housing is known as the **index line**, and it is at this point that you read (and set) your bearings.

Figure 14 |  *The protractor compass.*

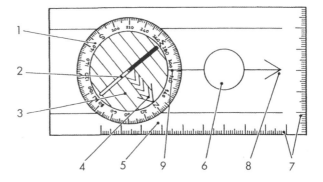

As I mentioned earlier, a compass suitable for mountain and moorland navigation should be designed in such a way that it performs a number of functions. The type described above fits the bill perfectly. Apart from finding north (by itself, not very useful), it can be used to work out accurate grid references and distances, to set the map in poor visibility, and to calculate precise bearings both from the map and from the ground. It can also be used to follow these bearings with a high degree of accuracy.

Although there are many different makes of compass available, the best tend to be those manufactured by Recta, Suunto, and Silva – the latter being the undisputed brand leader.

Photo 19 | *The protractor compass.*

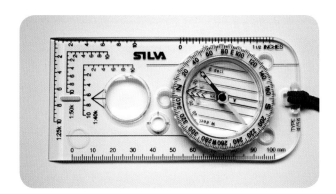

Sighting compasses

There are several different types of sighting compass available, the two most common being the **mirror compass** and the **optical sighting** (or **prismatic**) **compass**. The best of these share many of the characteristics of the protractor compasses described above – the most important being that they have a rotating compass housing with orienting lines, and a transparent base plate with romer scales and a magnifying lens.

Mirror compasses have a hinged lid over the housing that lifts to reveal a mirror. In use, you hold the compass just below eye level with the mirror open in such a way that it reflects the needle and the orienting arrow. In this position you can sight on objects and read (and set) bearings accurately. However, some models have base plates that are opaque which is not helpful when taking bearings from the map, and others have base plates that are too small and/or lack magnifying lenses and romer scales.

Standard prismatic compasses, whilst extremely accurate, are also heavy and suffer from the disadvantage that they lack a base plate. The optical sighting compass, however, is a unique combination of a prismatic compass and a protractor compass, which makes it ideal for our purposes. Manufactured by Silva, at first glance it looks almost exactly like that shown in Figure 14 and Photo 19, but on further examination you will find that the needle has been replaced by a transparent swivel dial, and the compass housing is domed, and contains a lens and a small prism. This combination allows you to calculate bearings from the map, to sight extremely easily on objects and features, and to set and follow bearings to an accuracy of +/- 0.5°. In terms of mountain and moorland navigation, this instrument is top of the range.

The larger figure shows the forward bearing, whilst the smaller figure shows the back bearing (see Chapter 15 and Figure 25).

Photo 20 | *The view through the sighting window of an optical sighting compass. Compare this to Photo 25 (page 98).*

Getting the right balance

All the compasses described so far work by using the earth's magnetic field, and are based upon the principle that the north-seeking end of a revolving magnetic needle will always try to point directly towards magnetic north. However, there is considerable regional variation in the direction of the lines of magnetic force. In the most basic terms, these lines are vertical at the magnetic poles and horizontal at the equator, and as a consequence, the north-seeking end of the magnetic needle tends to dip in areas lying between the poles and the equator. In practice, this means that the needle has to be balanced in order that it does not foul on the base of the compass housing.

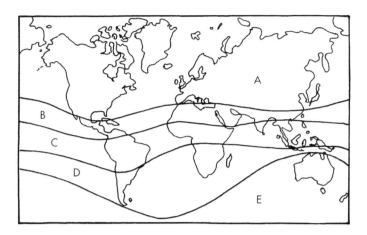

Figure 15 | Global magnetic zones.

The problem for compass manufacturers is that the balance point of the needle differs according to the latitude in which the compass will be used. In an attempt to address this problem, the compass industry has divided the earth into five **magnetic zones**, as illustrated in Figure 15. As you can see, the boundaries of these zones do not follow any logical or mathematical pattern, so the zones are fairly arbitrary. As a result, even where there are differences within a country, the whole country tends to be included within a single zone. However, if you use a compass calibrated for one zone in another zone, the further you travel from the correct zone, the more the needle will tilt, and in extreme cases, it can even stick. For this reason, a compass calibrated for use in the UK (northern hemisphere) will be unreliable if used, for example, in the Patagonian Andes (southern hemisphere).

When you buy a compass in the UK, you will always get one that is calibrated to work in zones A & B (the magnetic north zone), so there should not be a problem unless you intend to go to equatorial regions or the southern hemisphere. Even then, the increasing availability and popularity of global travel has resulted in some compass manufacturers designing compass models that effectively divide the world into two magnetic zones (the northern hemisphere and the southern hemisphere), and northern hemisphere compasses will work a considerable distance into the southern hemisphere, and vice versa. Additionally, it is possible to buy globally balanced compasses that will work in all magnetic zones – although it has to be said that these are not quite so accurate as the zone-specific models.

Although such considerations need not concern you when walking anywhere north of the Tropic of Cancer, if you intend to go on expedition to the far-flung reaches of the globe, particularly in equatorial regions or the southern hemisphere, you should get advice from a specialist retailer or one of the major compass manufacturers. If you are reading this book outside of the UK, similar considerations apply – for example compasses bought in New Zealand will be calibrated for the southern hemisphere and you will need to get a different compass if you intend to visit the northern hemisphere.

Electronic and digital compasses

I am going to make a distinction here between GPS devices (described below), which give positional information (and usually a lot more besides), and electronic or digital compasses, which give only directional information, and of which there are several types currently available. For example, many of the more sophisticated watches and altimeters incorporate electronic compasses, and a variety of compass apps are available for smart phones, some of which are significantly better than others. Whilst these types of compass may be useful for general direction finding, many are accurate only to within +/- 5°, which is significantly less accurate than a traditional protractor compass. Further disadvantages include the fact that electronic compasses have no facility for you to measure a bearing directly from the map; nor do they have romer scales or magnifying lenses. Additionally, with some models you need to be moving in order for the compass to work.

Having said this, the ever-increasing acceleration in the development of modern technology makes it virtually certain that new models will have appeared in the period between my writing these words and you reading them! Currently, the only plus points that I can see are that some have a memory that allows you to store bearings, whilst others not only warn you when you are off-course, but also tell you in which direction you have to go in order to get back on course. Personally, I still prefer a good old-fashioned reliable mechanical compass!

GPS devices

There are few things more likely to spark an argument between hillwalkers than mention of GPS devices. These clever hi-tech gadgets come in a variety of shapes and sizes, and work by using a network of satellites orbiting the earth to calculate such things as your position, speed, altitude, and direction of travel. Although the basic features tend to be fairly similar, there are some significant differences between the available models. For example, the more basic

models may not have compass or altimeter functions, and may have limited memory for storing route information, whilst the more advanced models are **map enabled** (you can download maps and routes into the device and then view them on the screen). There are also an increasing number of smart phone apps available, some of which are very useful – but none are a substitute for more traditional navigation techniques using paper map and hand-held compass.

Whilst I am on record as saying that I am not a fan of these hi-tech gadgets, technology has advanced and accuracy is now much improved. Because of these changes, I have altered my opinion (slightly!), and I now believe that the GPS system does have its uses so far as mountain and moorland navigation is concerned. However, I also believe that these devices are commonly misused, and that they encourage an over-reliance on gadgetry at the expense of good map interpretation and basic navigation techniques.

To my mind, the biggest advantage of GPS devices is that they give the user the opportunity to obtain useful additional information which can be of help when navigating in poor visibility or across featureless terrain. They can also be used to track your progress and to memorise your route so you can later download this onto a computer to see exactly where it was you went! Conversely, the biggest disadvantage is that it is easy to be beguiled by the technology and see a GPS device as a substitute for map interpretation and standard 'mechanical' compass techniques. In fact, despite the advances that have been made, these devices are still neither as consistently accurate nor as reliable as standard navigation techniques, and should never be used as a stand-alone navigation tool.

The uses and abuses of GPS devices are discussed in more detail in Chapter 18.

To recap

Of all the many different types of compass on the market, it is the protractor (or orienteering) compass which is the most useful for our purposes. In addition to indicating general direction, this can also be used to calculate and follow precise bearings both from the map and from the ground, and to facilitate the accurate measurement of grid references and distances. The magnifying lens in the base plate is also extremely useful.

Sighting models are available, and some of these are excellent, particularly the optical sighting compass, which shares all the advantages of a protractor compass with the extreme accuracy of a prismatic compass.

Electronic and digital compasses are being developed all the time, but currently suffer from several disadvantages, not the least of which is that they are not as accurate as sighting compasses, and they cannot be used to calculate bearings from the map.

GPS devices (including smart phone apps) are useful tools which can give the experienced user additional information which may be of help in extreme situations. However, there is a danger that the inexperienced user will become over-reliant on the technology which, despite claims to the contrary, is neither infallible nor a substitute for good map interpretation and route selection.

11 BEARINGS – INVISIBLE LINES

The most important feature of the protractor compass is that it allows you to calculate accurate bearings both from the map and from the ground, and then to follow those bearings with a high degree of accuracy. In this chapter, we are going to look at how you calculate the bearings. We will discuss how you follow the bearings in the next chapter.

A bearing is simply an invisible straight line. A compass is an instrument that shows you where these invisible straight lines run – both on the ground and on the map. Make no mistake about it – modern protractor compasses are precision instruments, and when used correctly to follow a bearing they will take you precisely to where you want to go. However, in order for them to do that, you have to use them with precision. 'Roughly' is not good enough!

As with any new technique, you may find the procedures described below a little confusing or unwieldy to begin with, but (as with all the other techniques described in this book) once you have mastered the basic principles you will find calculating bearings very simple. To begin with, it is really important that you understand the basic principles at work, rather than the detail – in other words, you need to understand why you are doing what you are doing. Once you understand these basic mechanisms, everything else will fall into place very easily.

Let us look first at the way in which you can work out bearings from the map.

Grid bearings – invisible lines on the map

Because the compass housing rotates within the base plate and both the housing and the base plate contain sets of parallel lines, you can use your compass as a protractor. A protractor is simply a device for measuring angles (just like the protractor in a geometry set). I have said that a bearing is simply an invisible straight line, but what we are interested in is the direction in which that line runs. Direction is meaningless unless it is relative to something else, and in navigation we always work out directions relative to north, so the figure that relates to a bearing is simply the angle between two invisible straight lines – one going from the point at which you are going to start walking to where you want to go, the other going from the same start point to north. Convention has it that all bearings in land navigation are quoted in degrees east of north – in other words, you always measure the angle in a clockwise direction. This is shown clearly in Figure 16.

Let us assume that you wish to travel from point A to point B, and that point B is out of sight, perhaps owing to poor visibility. In order to calculate the bearing, you must measure the angle between one invisible straight line running from point A (your start point) to point B (your destination), and another invisible straight line running from point A to north.

Figure 16 | *Bearings. A bearing is simply the angle between two invisible lines, and is always measured in a clockwise direction (i.e. in degrees east of north).*

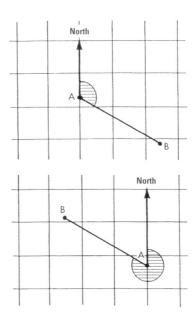

The first thing you must do is find the positions of both points A and B on the map. You must do this accurately. It is not enough to find their approximate positions – you must find their *precise* positions. If you understand the principle of scale, you should also appreciate this essential need for accuracy, for any error you make at this stage will be multiplied by the scale of the map. In other words, if you are using a 1:50,000 scale map, any error you make whilst taking your bearing from the map will be multiplied 50,000 times when you use it on the ground!

Until you are comfortable with the technique, you should use five distinct stages when taking a bearing from the map. With practice, this can be reduced to three, and after several years' experience, you will find that the procedure becomes almost one continuous movement.

Stage 1

Once you have found both positions as accurately as you can, place your compass on the map in such a way that the DOT arrow points in the direction in which you wish to travel (in this case, from A to B). Except when setting your map with your compass (see Chapters 7 and 12), you always *ignore the compass needle* when using the compass on the map.

Stage 2

Having made sure that the DOT arrow is pointing in the right direction, adjust the position of the compass until one of the parallel lines in the base plate (or one side of base plate) runs precisely between the two points. If your compass permits, it is always preferable to use one of the lines in the base plate rather than one of the sides, simply because it is easier to be more accurate. If your base plate is the recommended length (between 10 centimetres and 12.5 centimetres) and you find that the lines are not long enough to stretch between the two points, then you are trying to travel too far for a single leg of navigation and should try to find another, closer feature as your destination (see also Chapter 22).

Your compass should now be in a position such that, were you to run a pencil along one side of the base plate, the resulting straight line would run parallel to an imaginary straight line joining points A and B (or, if you have lined up the side of the base plate between the two points, this line would join points A and B). This is shown clearly in the upper part of Figure 17.

Figure 17 | *Calculating*
a grid bearing.
Top – stages 1 & 2:
line up the base plate.
Bottom – stages 3 & 4: line
up the orienting lines.

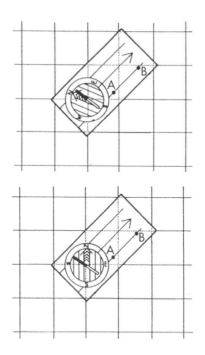

Stage 3

Once everything is lined up, and keeping the base plate firmly and accurately in position (something that can be very difficult to do whilst standing on the side of a wet and windswept hill!), turn the compass housing until the orienting arrow is pointing towards the northern (top) edge of the map. Remember, you should *ignore the compass needle* throughout this procedure.

Stage 4

Still keeping the base plate firmly in position, look for the nearest grid line that runs from the top to the bottom of the map, and turn the compass housing slightly until the orienting lines are exactly parallel to this north-south grid line. You will be most accurate if you can see a grid line close to one of the longer orienting lines, and you may find that you have to slide the base plate along the imaginary line between the two points, or even start again and use a different line in the base plate in order for this to occur. The resulting position is shown in the lower part of Figure 17 and in Photo 22. Check that the line in (or side of) the base plate is still accurately lined up between points A and B.

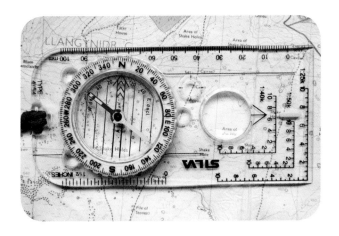

Once everything has been lined up accurately, you can take the compass off the map. What you have just done is used your compass as a protractor to measure the angle between two imaginary straight lines – one going from A to B (as shown by the lines in the base plate), the other going from A to north (as shown by the orienting lines). The angle is indicated by the figure at the index line – where the line containing the DOT arrow intersects the numbered segments on the compass housing. Remember that each segment around the compass represents 2°. You should aim to be accurate to within 1°.

The figure you now have is known as a **grid bearing** because it is an angle calculated using the grid lines that run from the bottom to the top of your map. At the top of the map, these grid lines all point towards a position known as **grid north**.

When using this technique, the most common mistakes tend to involve 90° errors, or multiples thereof! If, for example, you line everything up but the DOT arrow is pointing towards point A rather than point B, the resulting bearing will be 180° out! In this situation, most people's sense of direction will tell them that something is wrong. Worse, however, is if you mistakenly line up the orienting lines with the east-west grid lines, for you will then be either 90° or 270° out. In this situation, your sense of direction may not be good enough for you to realise that you have made an error. If, for example, you had calculated this bearing to take you parallel to the top of a line of cliffs, when you come to follow your bearing your error will result in you heading straight towards the edge! This is one reason that the orienting lines on the better compasses have their northern half coloured red and their southern half coloured black – it is simply there to remind you not to make a 90° error!

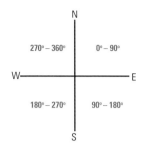

| 270° – 360° | 0° – 90° |
| 180° – 270° | 90° – 180° |

N
W——————E
S

Figure 18 | *Checking the quadrants.*

Before moving on to the next stage, it is a good idea to get into the habit of double-checking your bearing by looking at the map and working out roughly what the angle should be. Most people can judge angles to within 20° or so, and it will help if you use a technique called **checking the quadrants**. To do this, look at point A and imagine that the grid lines cross directly over this point. Any bearing that heads into the area enclosed by the northerly and easterly lines must be between 0° and 90°; any bearing that heads into the area enclosed by the easterly and southerly lines must be between 90° and 180°, and so on (see Figure 18).

Stage 5

The bearing you have obtained has been calculated relative to grid north – that is, the position to which the grid lines point. Before you can use this bearing on the ground, however, you need to convert it from a grid bearing into a **magnetic bearing**, as described next.

Magnetic variation – map to ground

What you have measured with your compass is the angle between two imaginary straight lines on your map – one going from point A to point B; the other going from point A to grid north. In making this calculation, you have used the north-south grid lines to show you where north lies. The problem is that when you come to use this information on the ground, there are no grid lines! – therefore it becomes necessary for you to find north using some other means. The most convenient method is to use the needle of your compass.

So far so good. Unfortunately, however, your compass needle does not point to grid north, but to magnetic north, which is in a different place! This is due to two separate factors. Firstly, the map is flat whereas the earth is curved; secondly, the magnetic field of the earth is moving relative to the geographic north pole (also known as **true north**). The difference in angle between grid north and magnetic north is known as the **magnetic variation**, and owing to the nature of the earth's magnetic field, this alters from place to place and from year to year. All OS and BMC/Harvey maps have the magnetic variation for that area printed in the key, together with the rate of annual change. Although this rate of change is very small, you should always check it and adjust the magnetic variation accordingly. Always round the resulting figure up or down to the nearest whole degree.

As it happens, the magnetic variation in Britain is currently (2016) tiny, varying between about 0° and 2° west of grid north, depending on the area, and decreasing by about 1° every 6 years. An error of 2° over a distance of 1km will result in you being just under 35 metres off target. The practical upshot of this is that you can ignore the effects of magnetic variation in the British Isles until about 2030 – as long as you keep your legs of navigation short (say to within no more than about 500 metres)! However, there are places in the world where the magnetic variation is much bigger, so I would not be doing my job properly if I did not explain how you should adjust your bearings accordingly.

The procedure by which you convert your grid bearing into a magnetic bearing is very straightforward. Assuming a westerly variation, all you need do is *add* the magnetic variation as illustrated in Figure 19. If, for example, you have a grid bearing of 126° and the magnetic variation is 3°W, your magnetic bearing will be 129°. So long as the magnetic variation is west of grid north (as it is currently in the UK) adding the magnetic variation to a grid bearing will always give you the corresponding magnetic bearing. This is because the magnetic needle will point to the west of grid north, so you need to take into consideration the fact that the angle will be larger. It is worth going over this again and referring to Figure 19 until you understand why you are doing what you are doing. Once you understand the principle, you will realise that if you go to somewhere like Yosemite in the US where there is an easterly magnetic variation, you will need to *subtract* the variation rather than add it.

To be accurate, before using any grid bearing on the ground, you need to adjust it on your compass to take account of magnetic variation, and the easiest way to do this is to turn the housing in an anticlockwise direction (for a westerly variation) or a clockwise direction (for an easterly variation) until the required number of degrees has been added or subtracted, remembering that each segment represents 2°. As an added check, it is a good idea to do the calculation in your head as well, for in the heat of the moment, it is very easy to add, say, 3 segments instead of 3°. Indeed, it is wise to get into the habit of double- (or even treble-) checking everything you do in poor visibility navigation!

You will find that calculating a bearing from the map when sitting comfortably in front of a table becomes straightforward after a few attempts. However, trying to do the same procedure when crouching on a windswept hillside in driving rain or snow can be a totally different proposition, but it is in exactly this type of situation when you need to be accurate. Bearing this in mind, it is not a bad idea, whenever possible, to calculate a few general magnetic bearings the night before a walk and make note of them on some form of **route card** (see Chapter 19).

Figure 19 | *Magnetic variation.*

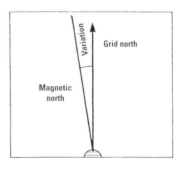

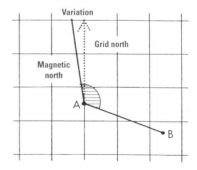

Magnetic bearings – invisible lines on the ground

Although the most common use for your compass will be taking bearings from the map and then following them on the ground, you can also use your compass to measure a bearing on the ground and then transfer this information onto your map. This can be useful in a number of ways, as will be described in more detail in Chapter 15.

As an example, let us assume that you are going to take a bearing on a noticeable feature on the near horizon using a standard protractor compass. Start by holding the compass in front of you, fairly close to your body and between waist and chest height, and with the DOT arrow pointing directly away from you (see Photo 23). This is the same position as that used when following a bearing, as will be described in the next chapter. Once you are holding the compass correctly, keep pointing the compass directly away from you and turn your whole body around until the DOT arrow points directly towards the noticeable feature; then – *without moving the base plate* – slowly turn the compass housing until the orienting arrow lies directly below the red end of the magnetic needle.

What you are doing is measuring the angle between an invisible straight line running between your position and the noticeable feature (via the DOT arrow), and another invisible straight line running from your position to magnetic north (via the magnetic needle). If you understand how magnetic variation works, and assuming a westerly variation, you will realise that you will need to *subtract* the magnetic variation from this bearing before you can use the information on your map (you will need to convert the **magnetic bearing** into a **grid bearing**). There are several ways in which this information can be used on a map, all of which are described in Chapter 15.

Photo 23 | *Holding the compass to take a magnetic bearing.*

There is one adaptation of this technique that does not require you to adjust for magnetic variation. Let us suppose that you are walking across some trackless terrain when you notice the cloud rolling in. In the distance, you can see a feature that you can identify on the map, but you realise that you have insufficient time to reach it before the cloud reaches you. If you quickly sight on the feature using your compass and turn the compass housing to get the magnetic bearing, you can then follow this bearing to the feature as you would any other bearing (as described in the next section) even when that feature becomes obscured by the cloud. Please note, however, that you must start to follow the bearing immediately, and not stray off course.

If you are using an optical sighting compass, the procedure is even easier, for all you need do is look through the sighting window and read off the bearing to the nearest degree.

To recap
Bearings are simply invisible straight lines, and your compass is simply an instrument that shows you where these invisible straight lines run across the landscape.

Grid bearings are invisible straight lines on the map, whereas magnetic bearings are invisible straight lines on the ground. Before you can use a grid bearing on the ground (or a magnetic bearing on a map), you need to convert it to take account of the magnetic variation.

Assuming a westerly variation (as currently [2016] exists in the UK), when you convert a bearing from Grid to Mag, you add – whereas when you convert from Mag to Grid, you get rid! With an easterly variation (such as in the US and parts of Europe), the opposite applies.

12 PUTTING IT ALL TOGETHER

Calculating accurate bearings from the map is of little use unless you can follow them accurately on the ground in all weather conditions. Before we look at the ways in which you can do this, it is important to consider a couple of other factors.

As we have seen, your compass works by using the lines of force of the earth's magnetic field to attract one end of a magnetised needle. There are two potential problems with this. First, in some areas there are **magnetic anomalies** that upset the local magnetic field, and this will obviously have a knock-on effect on the accuracy of your compass. These anomalies are far more common than is generally believed, although many are so small as to cause a negligible effect on your compass. Of the stronger ones, some are well documented (such as that in the Black Cuillin on Skye), whereas others are less well known. There are, for examples, anomalies in Borrowdale in the Lake District, and in the Carneddau in Snowdonia. Magnetic anomalies are not mentioned on OS or BMC/Harvey maps, but may be mentioned in the better local guide books. This having been said, and bearing in mind the comments below, you should always trust your compass, as its sense of direction will almost invariably be better than yours! It is far easier to blame a magnetic anomaly for being off route than to admit to human error, but the latter is far more likely!

Second, some 'magnetic anomalies' are man-made! Anything metallic or magnetic has the potential to affect the compass needle if the two come close enough, so be aware of metallic objects whenever you are using a compass. Items that commonly cause problems are mobile phones in breast pockets, and digital or auto-focus cameras worn around the neck or placed inside a map pocket. Even under-wired bras can have an effect if the compass is held too close. I once asked a person being assessed to set his map with his compass whilst standing by a metal gate. He rested his map on the gate and then placed his compass on top, at which point the needle lined up along the top bar of the gate!

When used correctly to follow an accurately calculated bearing, your compass will take you *precisely* to where you want to go. However, I need to issue a word of caution. Sometimes strange things happen to our sense of direction when we follow a compass, and most people who walk regularly will sooner or later experience a nagging conviction that their compass is lying! This will usually be in poor visibility, and often when getting the bearing right is vital. The temptation will be to give in to this conviction and ignore the compass, but that is the worst thing you can do. By all means double- or even treble-check your bearing and get your companions to do the same, but if you keep on getting the same result, it is an odds-on certainty that your sense of direction is at fault, not the compass! This has happened to me a few times, the worst being in abysmal visibility in winter conditions, and in a situation where getting the bearing right was critical. I was in an area I knew well, and whilst every molecule in my body told me I had to go one way, my compass told me I had to go in a totally different direction. I double-checked everything (twice!), I even closed my eyes and turned around a few times in an attempt to disorientate myself, but this made no difference. It was a really difficult decision to follow the compass, but that is what I did – and a few worried minutes later, I ended up precisely where I had intended.

Following bearings

There are two methods you can use to follow a bearing. Both require concentration and discipline; neither should be haphazard or slapdash. The first method, **spotting**, is the more difficult of the two, but it is an essential skill to master because it is the only method you can use to follow a bearing accurately if you are alone. It is therefore important that you are familiar with the process and have practised it before you need it for real. The second technique, **leapfrogging**, is somewhat more straightforward, but it still requires practice if you are to use it accurately and efficiently. Indeed, I cannot over-emphasise how important it is for you to practise both these techniques. You cannot become efficient and effective at navigation unless you are familiar with all the techniques, and this requires regular practice.

Spotting

Let us assume you are standing at point A and wish to follow a bearing to point B, which is out of sight. You have calculated the bearing from the map, adjusted it for magnetic variation, and it is set on your compass. Assuming you are using a standard protractor compass, you must now hold your compass in front of you in as horizontal a position as possible, with the DOT arrow pointing directly away from you and the base plate between about 15 and 30 centimetres below your chin. Keep it level, and keep it centred – in other words, a line running from the DOT arrow, back through the index line (the point where you read the bearings), and on through the pivot of the needle, should pass through the centre-line of your body. Once in this position, lock your arm so that the compass effectively becomes an extension of your body, moving with you as you turn. Now, *without moving the compass housing*, slowly turn around until the *red* end of the needle lies directly over the orienting arrow. The DOT arrow will now be pointing precisely to point B.

There are a couple of points worth noting. First, because the compass needle is balanced on a pivot, you should always make sure that you hold your compass horizontally, for otherwise the needle may foul in the housing and not turn cleanly. Second, because the movement of the needle is damped, you should always give it time to settle into the correct position before using a magnetic bearing. You are bound to be inaccurate if the needle is still swinging about, however gently, so get into the habit of counting to five each time you raise the compass into the sighting position.

Photo 24 | *Sighting along the DOT arrow when following a bearing.*

Once the red end of the needle is directly over the orienting arrow, you now need to imagine that the DOT arrow is showing you the direction of an invisible straight line that extends from the pivot of the compass needle, along the line of the DOT arrow, and on across the ground, all the way to your destination. In order to follow this invisible line, you must sight along it and look for some obvious or recognisable object such as an isolated tussock or an oddly shaped rock, which lies directly on this invisible line. Although this may sound simple, finding suitable objects can be extremely difficult, but it is vital that the object is something you can easily recognise, even after you have walked a few paces towards it and, perhaps, glanced at your feet to avoid tripping. It is, for example, inadvisable to choose a boulder on a scree slope, although there may well be occasions when you are forced to choose such an object, simply because it is the only thing available. Make sure, also, that your chosen object will not move – there are many stories about people taking sightings on sheep in the mist! Concentration and focus are essential – you may one day find yourself in a position where you have to sight, quite literally, on a clump of heather, a blade of grass, or even a ripple in the snow.

It is important that you keep the distance between each 'spot' short – never further than about 50 metres, even in the best visibility. The greater the distance between the spots, the more likely you are to lose sight of the object, and the greater will be any resulting error. Indeed, the most common mistake made by even experienced people is to leave too great a distance between each spot.

Once you have found a suitable, static object that lies directly on the invisible straight line, you can lower your compass and simply walk to that object. Once there, you repeat the procedure, and so on until you reach your destination.

One of the great advantages of spotting is that you are not forced to walk in a straight line, concentrating on your compass all the while. Once you have identified your object, you can walk to it via the easiest or most practical route. You can, for example, zigzag up or down steep slopes, bypass obstacles such as small pools or particularly evil-looking patches of bog, and even wander along the banks of a stream until you find a suitable crossing point. It does not matter where you go or how you get there, so long as you eventually reach the object on which you sighted, at which point you will be back on course. This is another reason why each spot should be chosen with care, for you may eventually approach it from a slightly different direction from which it might not be as obvious as you first thought.

If you use a sighting compass, the technique is the same except that you hold the compass in a slightly different way. The trick with the optical sighting compass is to hold it fractionally below eye level, with the base plate resting against the top of your cheek bone. In this position you can look through the prism window to see the hairline that indicates the bearing, yet also look over the top of the compass housing in order to see objects on the ground (see Photo 25). In this way, you can 'balance' objects on top of the hairline, giving you an accuracy of +/- 0.5°.

Photo 25 | *Using an optical sighting compass.*

Leapfrogging

You will quickly find that the biggest problem with spotting is finding suitable spots. If you are walking with one or more companions, you will find it much easier to use them as ready-made objects! However, whilst the technique is very simple, it does require practice if you are to do it smoothly and with the minimum of delay.

Having calculated your bearing, you should then send one of your companions off in front of you, heading in roughly the right direction, until either they are a few metres before the limit of visibility, or they have covered a distance of 50 metres (whichever is the smaller distance). Even in good visibility, they should never be more than 50 metres away from you. Once they have travelled the distance, they should turn around and face you, at which time you sight along the compass in the normal way, and move the person to the right or left until they are standing on the invisible line that marks your course. The whole party can now move to that position, at which point the procedure is repeated. In order to be accurate, it is essential that you take each successive sighting from the precise position at which your companion was standing.

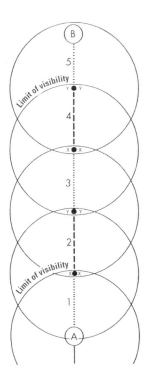

Figure 20 | Leapfrogging.

Shouting directions is not the best method of communication in this situation, for not only will wind and weather tend to conspire against you, but also when they are facing you, their left is your right, and vice versa. It is therefore easier, more effective and far less frustrating to use hand signals. Make big movements with your arms to move them to the left or right, fine-tune their position with smaller movements, then hold your arm straight up in the air to stop them when they are standing on the invisible line. Double-check their position before moving to them, and before you send them on in front, make absolutely certain that they know not to move once you have directed them to the correct point.

If there are two or more people with compasses, one can sight on the other, then walk past until the next limit of visibility is reached, and so on (hence the name of the technique). This procedure is illustrated in Figure 20. In this situation, it is also possible for the person acting as the 'spot' to double-check by using a **back bearing** as described in Chapter 15. If, as a result of sighting on a back bearing, the 'spot' person believes that their position is incorrect, he or she should move to what they believe is the correct position and the whole process starts again. The differences are seldom great (typically no more than a couple of metres), and the correct position can usually be agreed upon

Photo 26 | Following a
bearing by leapfrogging.

through compromise. If not, each person should double-check to make sure their compass is still set to the correct bearing, or that there is not something metallic or magnetic affecting one of the compasses. The important point in all of this is that one person must always remain on the invisible line.

Where the visibility and terrain allows, it is also possible to combine leapfrogging with **pacing** (see Chapter 14), thus killing two birds with one stone! In this instance, each person walks an identical agreed distance before stopping, in order that there is an ongoing awareness of the distance travelled.

Although, even with practice, leapfrogging can be extremely time-consuming, often doubling any estimate of time based upon standard speeds of travel, it does provide a very simple and straightforward means of navigating with extreme accuracy in all but the most severe conditions. However, it is important that you develop the ability to walk on a bearing using spotting – a skill that requires practice if you are to do it accurately.

'Walking on the needle'

In the most severe conditions such as whiteout, it may be impossible to use either of the techniques outlined above, simply because there are no spots on which to sight, and there is a risk you could become separated from your companions if you try to leapfrog. In this situation you will have to walk using only the direction shown by your compass – often referred to as 'walking on the needle'. This is a risky technique because unless you take great care, it is easy to walk at a slight angle to your intended course, slowly drifting onto a parallel bearing (see Chapter 22).

In terms of technique it is vital that you keep the DOT arrow on the compass pointing in your direction of travel but aligned with the centre of your body. People who hold the compass in their right hand tend to walk to the right of the bearing; people who hold the compass in their left hand tend to walk to the left of the bearing. This is because they hold the compass in a comfortable position rather than cocking their wrist slightly to keep the DOT arrow lined up.

One way to reduce this risk is to have two people follow the same bearing – one walking behind the other – so that the person at the rear can check that the person in front is not drifting. Every hundred metres or so, the person in front turns around and, if necessary, is guided back onto course by arm signals similar to those used in leapfrogging.

More about setting the map

Earlier in the book, I described how to set your map using map interpretation. In order to do this, you must be able to see one or more definite features, yet it is often extremely useful to set your map in poor visibility or in other situations where there are no definite features to which you can refer. In situations such as these, you can set your map using your compass. Although I have already described how to do this very simply by using the compass needle, there are a couple of other techniques that can be used, and these are particularly useful in those situations where you wish to set your map with greater accuracy.

First, set your compass to 0° so that the orienting arrow is in line with the DOT arrow, and the orienting lines in the base of the housing are parallel to the edges of the base plate. Next, holding the map flat, lay the compass on top in such a way that the edge of the base plate lies alongside a north-south grid line, and the DOT arrow points towards the northern (top) edge of the map. Now, keeping the base place firmly in position, turn the map and compass together, until the *red* end of the needle lies directly over the orienting arrow. Your map will now be set for most practical purposes, but if you wish to be totally accurate, you must take the magnetic variation into consideration.

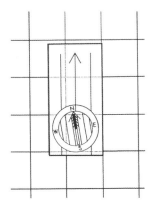

Figure 21 | *Setting the map with a compass.*

The easiest way to compensate for magnetic variation in this situation is to set the compass to the value of the variation. In other words, if the magnetic variation is 3° west, set your compass to 3° instead of 0°. What you are doing is following the same procedure as when you change a grid bearing to a magnetic bearing – adding the variation. When you have set the variation on your compass, follow the same procedure as before – lining up one side of the base plate alongside a north-south grid line with the DOT arrow pointing towards the northern edge of the map, then turning both map and compass together until the *red* end of the needle lies directly over the orienting arrow. This is shown clearly in Figure 21.

If you understand the principle of magnetic variation, you will realise that if the magnetic variation is 3° east, you need to set your compass for 357° (360° minus the variation). Remember – west is best; east is least.

Once your map is set correctly, you can get an accurate sense of direction by using line of sight. If you know your current position, you will be able to see in exactly which direction you need to walk to get to your objective, and unless the visibility is really poor, this may even be sufficient for you to reach your objective without having to use your compass to calculate and follow a bearing.

To recap

Whenever you use a compass, be aware of any metallic or magnetic objects that may affect its accuracy. This includes things such as mobile phones, cameras, and under-wired bras. This aside, you should always trust your compass as it will invariably have a better sense of direction than you!

There are three methods you can use to follow a bearing. Spotting involves finding objects that lie on the invisible line of the bearing, and is the only technique that can be used if you are alone. Finding suitable objects can be very difficult in poor visibility, and you will need to concentrate. With leapfrogging, you use your companions as the object, sending them ahead and then moving them to the left or right until they are standing on the invisible line of the bearing. Both techniques require regular practice if you wish to be accurate and efficient.

In particularly severe conditions, it may be impossible to find suitable spots, and leapfrogging may lead to the party becoming separated. In this situation, it will be necessary to 'walk on the needle', a difficult technique to master, and one that requires regular practice. This is more reliable if you have a companion to correct any drift.

You can also use your compass to set your map accurately if you cannot see enough features to do this by map interpretation.

PART 3 – ADDITIONAL TECHNIQUES

With only a little practice, you will soon begin to realise that your compass gives you a very accurate sense of direction. However, what it cannot do is tell you how far you have travelled, or how much further you have to go. Being able to access this type of information is very useful, especially in bad weather or poor visibility when it can be extremely difficult to gauge time and distance.

In this part of the book, we will look at a number of additional techniques that will be particularly useful when you find yourself in poor visibility or crossing featureless terrain. When used in combination with map interpretation, these merge together to encompass the art of **micro-navigation**.

13 ESTIMATING TIME

How long will it take?

Having the ability to estimate how long a walk (or part of a walk) will take is of obvious use and importance. We all do it (or should do it) to a certain extent when we plan our walks, even if only in terms of deciding whether our intended route is a half-day walk, a full-day walk, or a "let's take a tent" walk! Estimating to the nearest hour, however, is sometimes not accurate enough. If you are venturing into the mountains or across extensive areas of moorland, you really need to be able to estimate the duration of any leg of your walk to within a couple of minutes. Luckily, there is a simple way of doing this, based on a formula known as **Naismith's Rule**.

Let's start with the complicated stuff and then make it easier. In terms of general timing, Naismith's Rule states that a fit person will travel at an average of 5 kilometres per hour, and will take an extra 30 minutes for every 300 metres of ascent. This is useful as a general guide so long as you remember to take every metre of ascent into consideration, and to do this you need to be aware of the difference between **height gained** and **height climbed**. For example, you may ascend for 30 metres, descend for 20 metres, and then ascend again for a further 70 metres. Although you have only *gained* 80 metres of height, you have actually *climbed* 100 metres, and it is this full amount that must be taken into consideration. This is illustrated clearly in Figure 22 and Photo 27.

Quoted in the format above, Naismith's Rule is unwieldy and calculating timings for short distances tends to be a rather ponderous affair. However, if you break it down into smaller, more manageable units, you will find it far simpler to use. For example, 5 kilometres per hour is the same as 12 minutes per kilometre, which is the same as 6 minutes per 500 metres or just under one and a quarter minutes per 100 metres. However, there are several other factors to consider, not the least of which is that all but the fittest parties will find it difficult to maintain

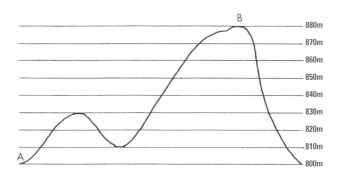

Figure 22 | Height gained
vs height climbed. From
A to B you gain 80 metres
but climb 100 metres.

a speed of 5km/hour during a long day in mountainous terrain. Additionally, in conditions of poor visibility and at other times when you are using micro-navigation techniques, you are almost certainly going to be moving more slowly. In practice, I have found that 4 or even 3 kilometres per hour is a far more accurate estimation of speed. Breaking this down gives us figures as below:

4km/hour = 15 minutes per kilometre = 1½ minutes per 100 metres.

3km/hour = 20 minutes per kilometre = 2 minutes per 100 metres.

2km/hour = 30 minutes per kilometre = 3 minutes per 100 metres.

If you measure the distance of any leg of navigation using your romer scale, and then use these 'chunked' figures, it is now relatively simple to estimate how long that leg going to take. If you remember just one figure related to estimating time, remember 1½ minutes per 100 metres. This estimate works surprisingly accurately in the vast majority of situations.

When estimating time, it is not sufficient simply to measure the distance on the map – you must also remember to take account of all ascents. Whilst this is mainly because most people take a slightly shorter pace (and therefore slow down) when they climb, it

Photo 27 | In order to reach
the summit in the distance,
you must first descend, and
this means that the height
climbed will be greater
than the height gained.

is also because unless the ground is perfectly flat, map distance and ground distance are different (although this has far less of an effect than many people believe). In order to make this additional calculation easy, you can break the rest of Naismith's Rule down as well – for example 30 minutes per 300 metres of ascent is the same as saying 1 minute for every 10 metres of ascent. If you recall what has been said about contour lines, you will remember that the vertical interval on OS maps (in hilly areas) is 10 metres, which means all you need do is look along the line you are going to walk, and add one extra minute for every uphill contour you cross. Simple! There are just three provisos. First, if you are using an Explorer map in flattish or lowland terrain, you should check to see whether the vertical interval is 10 metres or 5 metres as this will obviously make a difference. Second, if you are using a BMC or Harvey map, you should add 1½ minutes per contour line as the vertical interval on these maps is 15 metres. Third, whilst short or shallow descents can usually be ignored, you will need to add about 5 minutes for every 100 metres of height lost where the descent is steep or exceptionally long.

The speed at which you walk will be affected by a number of variables, including your fitness (and the fitness of the rest of your party), the nature of the terrain, weather conditions, weight of rucksack, and any long, steep ascents or descents. For example, you will almost certainly be slower at the end of a long day than at the beginning, slower crossing boggy ground than when on a good path, slower when backpacking than when on a half-day walk, and slower when heading into the wind than when walking with it behind you. What you must always bear in mind is that Naismith's Rule is purely a *guide* to the time you will take, not a hard and fast rule. Your estimate must therefore be adjusted according to the prevailing conditions. It must also be adjusted to take account of the navigation techniques you are using. In practice, it is useful to work on the basis that you will walk at 4km/hour under most circumstances where micro-navigation is being used, at 3km/hour where you are spotting, and at 2km/hour where you are leapfrogging.

There are a number of mind-boggling formulae (of which **Tranter's Variations** are probably the most widely known) that allow you make some of these adjustments mathematically. Whilst there is nothing wrong with using these should you feel the desire (assuming, of course, you can use them without the aid of a laptop), most experienced walkers rely on their experience. Apart from being far less complicated, this is also often far more accurate!

More useful, however, is a **speed/time grid**, as shown in Figure 23. This allows you not only to work out a time based on the expected speed, but also to get an idea of the likely error factors if you walk slightly faster or slower. In effect, what you are going to do is to use the **speed/time grid** to work out a **time window**. For example, let's assume you are heading towards a

ESTIMATING TIME

					HORIZONTAL DISTANCE (metres)					
		100	150	200	250	300	350	400	450	500
SPEED (Km/hr)	5	1'15"	1'50"	2'25"	3'00"	3'35"	4'10"	4'50"	5'25"	6'00"
	4.5	1'20"	2'00"	2'40"	3'20"	4'00"	4'40"	5'20"	6'00"	6'40"
	4	1'30"	2'15"	3'00"	3'45"	4'30"	5'15"	6'00"	6'45"	7'30"
	3.5	1'40"	2'35"	3'25"	4'20"	5'10"	6'00"	6'50"	7'45"	8'35"
	3	2'00"	3'00"	4'00"	5'00"	6'00"	7'00"	8'00"	9'00"	10'00"
	2.5	2'25"	3'35"	4'50"	6'00"	7'10"	8'25"	9'35"	10'50"	12'00"
	2	3'00"	4'30"	6'00"	7'30"	9'00"	10'30"	12'00"	13'30"	15'00"
	1.5	4'00"	6'00"	8'00"	10'00	12'00"	14'00"	16'00"	18'00"	20'00"

All timings rounded up or down to nearest 5 seconds

VERTICAL DISTANCE:

On OS Maps   Add one minute for every uphill contour crossed

On Harvey Maps   Add 1'30" for every uphill contour crossed

Figure 23 | *Speed/time grid.*

pool, a distance of 350 metres away, in thick mist. You are going to follow a compass bearing, and are going to use the spotting technique described in Chapter 12. You therefore estimate that you will walk at 3km/hour, which means you should reach the pool after 7 minutes. This becomes your **optimum time** – the time at which you are most likely to reach your target. What you now do is look at the figure above this optimum time (6 minutes), and the figure below (8½ minutes). This gives you your time window. You now know that you can concentrate on your bearing for the first 6 minutes of this particular leg of navigation. After 6 minutes, you should start to be a little more observant because you must be nearing your objective, which – in ideal circumstances – you should reach after 7 minutes. However, if you haven't reached it after 7 minutes, you can continue until 8½ minutes have elapsed before starting to become concerned! If you haven't found your objective by the time the time window closes, you stop and take stock, rechecking your bearing and your distance calculations. Perhaps you have been particularly slow – maybe there was an awkward section that slowed you up, or your companion stopped to retie a boot lace!

Photo 28 | The nature
of the terrain will affect
your speed, even in good
visibility. Boulder-strewn
areas such as this will almost
certainly slow you down.

If you believe you may have been overly slow, you can continue to the next lowest figure (in this example, 10½ minutes), but if you still have not reached your objective, you must stop and rethink your position. It is all too easy to continue in the hope that your objective will magically appear. We will explore what to do if you find yourself in this situation in Part 4.

Accurate time estimation is thus a mixture of simple mathematics and experience. Naismith's Rule can be used to calculate an approximate duration; experience should then give you a reasonable estimate of your speed of travel and alert you as to whether to add or subtract a few minutes. Some people time themselves over known distances during a walk, then use a speed/time grid to work out their average speed; others work out a percentage error on the first few legs of the walk, and then use this to further adjust all later calculations that day. During long walks in difficult terrain, some experienced walkers take tiredness into consideration and increase their timings slightly towards the end of the day. You should adopt a method which best suits you, finding this method through trial, error and experience, and using Naismith's Rule as a starting point rather than the be-all and end-all of time estimation. Thus, as with all aspects of navigation, it is important that you practise estimating time whenever possible.

To recap

The ability to estimate the duration of any leg of navigation is an essential skill when venturing into the mountains or crossing extensive areas of moorland. A reasonably accurate estimation of time can be calculated by using Naismith's Rule, this estimate being made more precise by adding or subtracting time according to the conditions and the terrain.

A speed/time grid is useful as it eliminates the need for mental arithmetic, and allows immediate access to information about the size of likely errors caused by different speeds and distances. It can also be used to work out optimum times and time windows.

14 ESTIMATING DISTANCE

How far have I travelled?

If the estimation of time is an important part of poor visibility navigation, the estimation of distance plays an equally essential role. Indeed, many people find it far easier to be consistently accurate when estimating distance than when estimating time, and the simple **pacing** technique described below makes it a very accessible skill. However, distance estimation is a two-way process – not only is it useful to know how far you are going to travel between one objective and the next, it is also helpful if you can estimate, more or less precisely, how far you have travelled during any particular leg of navigation.

Estimating distances from the map is very simple. For a start, the grid lines on all the recommended maps are always exactly 1 kilometre apart, so this immediately gives you a rough guide to distance. However, in poor visibility, you really need to be far more precise, and this is where the scales on your compass base plate become useful.

If you have one of the recommended compasses, this will have a scale (or scales) in centimetres and millimetres, printed on the base plate. The better models will also have a special set of scales known as romer scales (often just called romers), the use of which is described below. Romers are extremely useful; but if your compass does not have one, you do not have to buy a new compass as they can be bought very cheaply as separate items (see also Figure 8).

You should remember from Chapter 6 that on 1:50,000 scale maps, 1mm represents 50 metres on the ground, on 1:40,000 scale maps, 1mm represents 40 metres, and on 1:25,000 scale maps, 1mm represents 25 metres. It is therefore a simple matter to use the scales on your compass base plate to measure distance. If you measure the distance between your present position and your objective, you will be able to obtain a reasonably precise figure for the length of that leg of your walk. Obviously, this will be most accurate when you are walking in a straight line, but the time when you need to be most accurate is when you are forced by the conditions or visibility to use compass bearings, and these, by their very nature, will force you to walk (more or less) in straight lines. If you are not walking in a straight line, but following a curving or meandering route, you can use the lanyard on your compass, lining it up along your route in order to get the distance.

Counting millimetres and doing even the simplest mental arithmetic in bad weather can be extraordinarily difficult! It is very easy to make mistakes so you will need to concentrate. Always either double-check your calculations or, even better, get a companion to do the same calculation and then compare the answers. If, however, you have access to a romer scale, your task will be far simpler, because romer scales do the mental arithmetic for you.

Photo 29 | *Using the romer on a compass base plate to measure distance. There is a small feature approximately 550 metres from the road.*

The 'standard' romer, such as that found on the larger compass base plates, has scales of 1:50,000, 1:40,000 and 1:25,000. Other compasses may have different scales, and some have a facility whereby you can interchange scales. In use, romers are simplicity itself – instead of reading off the distance in millimetres and then making the conversion, you simply read off the distance in metres. If your compass does not have this facility, you can either buy a separate romer scale, or even make your own along the lines shown in Figure 8 (draw this accurately on a piece of fairly stiff, white card then take it to a print shop and get it laminated). An added advantage is that, because these scales work on the principle of dividing grid squares into tenths, they can also be used as a means of giving quick and accurate grid references. This function can be very useful if you use a GPS device (see Chapter 18).

It is, of course, of little use working out the precise length of a particular leg of navigation from the map unless you can also put this information to good use on the ground. It may well be that you can judge *roughly* when you have walked one kilometre across flat and even ground in fine weather, but across a bare mountainside or trackless moorland, when you can see less than 50 metres in any direction and the wind is trying to blow you off your feet, *roughly* is not good enough. In any case, unless you have some definite point of reference, travelling 100 metres in bad weather can feel like walking one kilometre in fine conditions. It is in these types of situations that the technique of pacing comes into its own.

In order to use this technique, you need to calibrate your pace. To do this, find a measured length of exactly 100 metres (try your local sports centre or athletic track). Alternatively, if you can get hold of a 100 metre tape or two fairly new 50 metre climbing ropes you can measure the distance for yourself. Using your normal stride, and starting off with your right foot, walk the entire distance of 100 metres counting one pace every time your left foot touches the ground (in other words, count double paces), and then make a note of the number of paces you have taken. It is best to do this at least three or four times and then work out an average.

Alternatively, get someone who can already use the technique accurately to pace out the distance for you. In this instance, it is preferable for them to walk a distance of, say, three hundred metres. You then follow the same procedure as above, following the route they took, and then divide the number of double paces you have taken by (in this example) three to get your average number of paces per hundred metres. If you use this method, it is important that you let the person pace the distance first, and then follow it by yourself, for otherwise there is a danger that his pace will affect your pace (or vice versa!).

Whichever method you use, it is vital that you walk using your normal pace. Try not to think too much about what you are doing, and avoid exaggerating your stride. Once you have worked out how many paces you take to cover 100 metres, the information can be put to good use. If, for example, you take 65 paces per 100 metres, and your next leg of navigation is 400 metres in length, you know how many paces you must take before you will arrive at the objective.

Some people count single paces instead of double paces as described above. However, the double pace method is preferable simply because it involves smaller numbers. Additionally, pacing can be tedious at the best of times, and if there is any danger that you could you lose count because your concentration is disturbed, it is pointless you starting in the first place! The most effective and reliable method of pacing therefore involves counting in terms of hundreds of metres rather than hundreds of paces. In other words, you should divide your pace counting into 100 metre blocks, starting again from zero at the

Photo 30 | *Pacing is useful for measuring distance – but it's easy to lose your concentration, especially if walking with companions!*

start of each succeeding block. For example, if you are travelling a distance of 725 metres and you take 64 paces per 100 metres, do not multiply 64 by 7.25 (for reasons which should immediately be obvious!). Count to 64 once (100 metres covered), then start again from zero. Do this seven times and (in this example) your objective should be about 16 paces away. As it happens, if the visibility is poor, you should not be walking this far on a single leg of navigation, for reasons that are explained in Chapter 22.

Even using this method, however, it is easy to lose count of how many hundred metres you have covered. It is therefore a good idea to have some means by which you can record how far you have travelled. You can buy a small counting device (called a tachometer), which you fix onto the side of your compass base plate, and which allows you to record how many 100 metre blocks you have travelled. Simpler (and cheaper) is to use a handful of pebbles, twigs, boiled sweets, coins, etc. Using the example given above, you would hold seven objects in your hand, and after each 64 paces (100 metres), you put one in your pocket (or discard it). A further advantage of this method is that you always have a quick visual reference of how far you have yet to travel. Avoid the temptation to transfer objects from one hand to the other, because you may forget which hand is which!

Many people use toggles on a piece of cord (often the neck strap of their map case), moving one toggle up (or down) the cord after each 100 metre block. Personally, I do not like this technique as I keep on forgetting which way I should be moving the toggles! Be that as it may, the examples above are only suggestions. It is important that you find a method with which you feel happy and confident, which is infallible, and which works for you.

With only a small amount of practice, you will find that pacing is incredibly accurate, especially if you keep each leg of navigation as short as possible. The further you travel between known points, the more you will have to take into account a host of other factors, including the nature of the terrain, your physical fitness, whether you are carrying a heavy load or whether the wind is blowing directly against you, all of which are going to affect your length of stride. For example, on steep or very rough ground, most people will take shorter strides than usual, whereas on smooth, slightly down-sloping ground, the length of each stride is likely to increase. On very steep ground, pacing simply doesn't work … but it is often unnecessary in such circumstances as you will know precisely where you are on your bearing as soon as you reach a break of slope.

ESTIMATING DISTANCE

Number of paces away from target at 5% and 10% error (rounded up)

		HORIZONTAL DISTANCE (m = metres)								
		100m	150m	200m	250m	300m	350m	400m	450m	500m
	5%	5m	7.5m	10m	12.5m	15m	17.5m	20m	22.5m	25m
	58	3	4	6	7	9	10	12	13	15
	60	3	5	6	8	9	11	12	14	15
	62	3	5	6	8	9	11	12	14	16
	64	3	5	6	8	10	11	13	14	16
	66	3	5	7	8	10	12	13	15	17
% error/PACES	**68**	3	5	7	9	10	12	14	15	17
	70	4	6	7	9	11	13	14	16	18
	10%	10m	15m	20m	25m	30m	35m	40m	45m	50m
	58	6	9	12	15	17	20	23	26	29
	60	6	9	12	15	18	21	24	27	30
	62	6	9	13	16	19	22	25	28	31
	64	6	10	13	16	19	22	26	29	32
	66	7	10	13	17	20	23	26	30	33
	68	7	10	14	17	20	24	27	31	34
	70	7	11	14	18	21	25	28	32	35

Figure 24 | *Distance/ pace grid.*

The amount of adjustment needed in each situation obviously varies from person to person, just as the original number of paces will vary, and your personal amounts of variation can only be found through experience. Although the likely errors are generally less than people think, some people find a **pace/ distance grid** useful (see Figure 24) as it allows you to see the effects of 5% and 10% errors over various distances. It is also far easier to use than some of the complicated formulae that take into account such things as the angle of slope. In my experience, most people can pace to within about 7% in all but the most extreme conditions.

I am not trying to imply that you should count paces all the time, whenever you go hillwalking – far from it! In the same way that you should not have to rely on your compass in good conditions, all the additional techniques described in this part of the book should be considered secondary to your skills at map interpretation, and you should only need to use these techniques in poor conditions or when you are in featureless terrain. Having said this, they all demand practice in order to be accurate, so it is a good idea to use them occasionally in favourable conditions until you become proficient, and to keep practising them every now and then, just to keep your hand in.

To recap

It is extremely useful to be able to estimate accurate distances, especially when walking in conditions of poor visibility or across trackless terrain. Not only should you be able to estimate distances from the map, you should also be able to estimate the distance covered on the ground. This is best done through step counting or pacing.

A pace/distance grid is helpful as it allows quick and easy access to information about the likely effects of 5% and 10% errors.

15 MORE ABOUT BEARINGS

Once you have practised taking and following bearings a few times and have started to become familiar with the underlying mechanisms, you will begin to realise that their use is limited solely by your imagination. In this chapter, I want to look at a few of the more common and useful adaptations.

Using back bearings – 'walking onto a bearing'

When following a bearing from point A to point B, you line up the *red* end of the compass needle over the orienting arrow so that the DOT arrow points to point B. This is known as a forward bearing. If, however, you turn around 180° until the *white* end of the needle lines up over the orienting arrow, the DOT arrow will point back to point A. This is known as a **back bearing** (see Figure 25). Back bearings are useful in several ways, not the least of which is that they allow you to retrace your steps, because no matter where you are along your bearing, as long as one person stays on the invisible line, you can always get back to where you started (see also Chapter 24). They can also be used to double-check positioning when leapfrogging, as described in Chapter 12.

One extremely useful adaptation of back bearings is a technique known as 'walking onto a bearing'. Let us assume that you are in the middle of nowhere (point X in Figure 26) and you notice the mist is starting to roll in. You cannot see your objective (point B), but you can see a point you can identify on the map (point A). The first thing to do is use the map and compass in

Figure 25 (below) | *Back bearing.*

the usual way to calculate the grid bearing from point A to point B, then convert this to a magnetic bearing. What you now have set on your compass is the information relating to an invisible straight line that runs between point A and point B. If you were standing on that line and you lined up the *white* end of the needle over the orienting arrow (i.e. used a back bearing), the DOT arrow would point straight to point A, so in order to walk onto the bearing, all you need do is line up the *white* end of the needle over the orienting arrow, then move to the left or right until the DOT arrow points directly to point A, at which point you must be standing on the invisible line that runs between the two points. You can now turn around 180° and follow the forward bearing to point B in the normal way (see Figure 26). This technique can be extremely useful when used in conjunction with route cards (see Chapter 19).

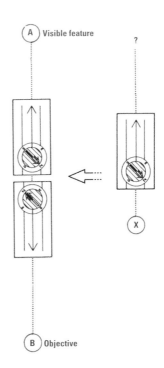

Figure 26 (right) | *'Walking onto a bearing' – the compass on the right of the drawing is set to a bearing between points A and B, calculated from the map. By sighting along a back bearing and moving to the left from point X until the DOT arrow points to point A, you have walked onto the bearing between points A and B. Once there, if you turn around 180° you can follow a forward bearing to Point B.*

Avoiding obstacles – boxing and dog-legging

Let us assume that you are walking in thick mist, following a bearing to a trig point that lies towards the far end of a spur that terminates in cliffs. You have measured the distance and are pacing (or keeping a note of time) as you do not want to overshoot. Some way along the bearing, you come across a particularly evil section of bog. If the visibility is good enough, you might be able to sight on a spot on the far side (as in spotting), or send a companion around and then sight on them (as in leapfrogging), but in both these cases you would lose the integrity of your pacing. The way around this problem is to use a **box bearing** (see Figures 27 and 28).

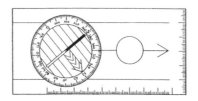

Figure 27 | *Compass set*
for a box bearing.

First, make a note of the number of paces (or minutes) that have been taken so far, and then decide whether it is better to detour around the obstacle to the left or to the right. This decision will obviously be affected by a number of factors, including the nature of the terrain (especially the proximity to any dangerous ground), and the nature and shape of the obstacle (as far as it is visible). Once you have made your decision, hold your compass in front of you in the normal way, then turn towards the chosen direction until the compass needle lines up as precisely as possible between the *east* and *west* marks on the compass housing (i.e. at right angles to the orienting lines as in Figure 27), at which point you will be facing 90° away from your original course. On many compasses, the northern half of the orienting lines are coloured red whilst the southern half are coloured black, and this will assist your accuracy. Indeed, some compasses also have a line across this mid-point. Now follow the new direction shown by the DOT arrow in the normal way, making sure you count your paces, until you find a place where you can get past the obstacle. Make a note of how many paces you took to reach this point, then pass the obstacle on your original bearing, continuing any distance or time estimations that you had been previously using. Once past the obstacle, turn 90° again, but this time in the *opposite direction* to that taken originally (e.g. if the red end of the needle was pointing towards *west*, make sure that it now points towards *east*), and follow this new direction for precisely the same number of paces as before. If you have been accurate, you will now be back on course again, but on the far side of the obstruction. This technique is often referred to as **boxing** (or **boxing around**) a feature, and is shown clearly in Figure 28.

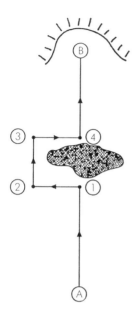

Using box bearings has several advantages over other techniques, not least being that it makes it unnecessary to move the compass housing. Additionally, although some people may argue that the technique cannot be accurate because it is difficult to line up the compass needle precisely between the east and west marks, in practice the distances involved are so small that the error factors have minimal effect. It should be obvious that if an obstacle is large enough to be shown on a map, you should calculate bearings around it in the usual way, rather than trying to avoid it using a box bearing.

Whilst using box bearings will be effective in most situations, sometimes the nature of the 'obstacle' is such that boxing is not the best option. A good example of this is shown in Figure 29. Let us assume that this is a winter scenario and the area in which you are walking is snow covered. A direct bearing from point A to point B will take you parallel to the edge of the cliff, and you are concerned that even if you are accurate in following a direct bearing, there is a danger (at two points in particular) that you might break through any cornice. You could box around these two points – indeed, you could box a large proportion of the route – but this would be time consuming and inefficient. In any case, there is an easier way!

Working on your map, draw a line from point A towards point B, but in such a way that it angles away from the direct route in order to avoid the 'dangerous' areas. Using your romer, measure a set distance along this line and mark a cross. Calculate the bearing of this line in the normal way, then follow this bearing for the distance you have measured. You will now be standing at point X on the ground, even though there is nothing there to confirm this. Now draw another line from point X to point B, measure the distance and calculate the bearing as normal, then follow this second bearing for the distance you have measured. This should take you safely to point B. This technique is known as dog-legging or using a dog-leg bearing.

Figure 28 | *Box bearing in action.*

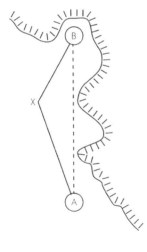

Figure 29 | *Dog-leg bearing.*

Having the ability to follow bearings and count paces means that any line you draw on a map, you can follow on the ground. It also means that any bearing you take on the ground can be drawn as a line on a map. The combinations and uses are therefore virtually limitless!

Crossing the line – using linear features

As was mentioned in Chapter 11, there are two types of bearing – grid bearings (bearings taken from the map), and magnetic bearings (bearings taken from the ground). Magnetic bearings can be useful in a number of ways, such as working out your position when walking along a linear feature such as a path or ridge. This is illustrated in Figure 30.

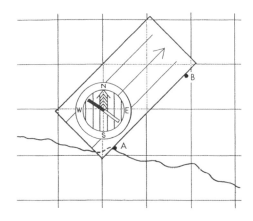

Figure 30 | *Location on a linear feature – by taking a bearing on a prominent feature (B) and then plotting it on the map, you can find your location on a linear feature (A).*

To do this, find a feature that you can identify both on the ground and on the map, and take a magnetic bearing on it as described in Chapter 11. Convert this to a grid bearing, then place the compass on the map in such a way that the orienting arrow is pointing to the top (northern) edge of the map with the orienting lines running parallel to the north-south grid lines, and one side of the base plate (or one of the lines in the base plate) is touching the feature on which you have just sighted. Your position will be where the same side of the base plate (or same line in the base plate) crosses the linear feature on which you are standing (see also Photo 23).

You can also use this technique in reverse. For example, if you are walking along a ridge (or other linear feature) and need to strike off at a particular point which is not obvious on the ground, you can use your map to work out the bearing of a distant object from the position at which you need to leave the ridge, set this on your compass, and then use this information to confirm when you have reached the correct position by regularly sighting on the distant object.

You will be at the correct position when the DOT arrow points directly to the distant object and the red end of the needle lies directly over the orienting arrow.

A similar procedure can be used to measure the direction of a linear feature on the ground, and then transfer this information to the map. For example Chapter 5 gave an instance of relocating by descending from a mountain to reach a forest boundary, following the edge of the forest until you come to a stream, and working out your position at this point. If there is more than one stream entering the forest, you can take a magnetic bearing along the line of the stream, convert this to grid, then put your compass on the map in such a way that the orienting arrow points to the top of the map with the orienting lines parallel to the north-south grid lines. At this point, the lines in the base plate (and, therefore, the sides as well) will be running parallel to the stream on which you took the bearing. This procedure can be used to measure the direction of any linear feature on the ground, and then transfer this information to the map.

Although using magnetic bearings in this way is undoubtedly useful, it can be argued that it is a good example of *overuse of the compass*. After all, if the visibility is good enough for you to take these bearings, you should be able to locate yourself on a linear feature by setting your map and using line of sight, as described in Chapter 7.

A classic example of using line of sight to get your location on a linear feature is that of using **transits**. For example, you may be following a path along a break of slope when you notice that a farm in the valley is directly in line with a trig point on the far side of the valley. In navigation terms, the farm and the trig point are said to be in *transit*. If you now draw a line on the map between the trig point and the farm, and continue it until it crosses the path, it will indicate your current position (see Figure 31).

Figure 31 | *Using transits.*
A = trig point.
B = farm.
X = your position.

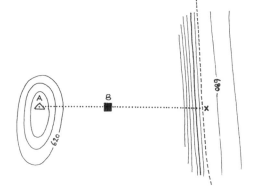

Making life easy – aiming off

Using bearings in conjunction with linear features is one of the most useful and simple of navigation techniques. Indeed, if you are heading towards a linear feature that you wish to use as a handrail (see Chapter 16), it is not strictly necessary to follow the bearing with precision because, as long as you head in roughly the right direction and the linear feature lies across your path, you are bound to reach it.

As has already been mentioned, the real art of poor visibility navigation is to keep everything as simple as possible by adhering to the KISS principle (see Chapter 22). For example, if your objective is suitable, it is often easier to aim deliberately to miss it! This technique, known as **aiming off** (or **aiming away**), can be used when the point for which you are making lies on, or very close to, a linear feature such as a stream, track, long field boundary, or noticeable break of slope. If, for example, you are heading for a stream junction, you will find it is easier to reach if you deliberately aim either upstream or downstream of the exact point. The logic here is simple; assuming the stream lies more or less across your path, as long as you head towards it, you are bound to cross it. However, any slight error you make when following your bearing will cause you to miss the junction, so when you arrive at the stream, you will have no idea whether the junction lies upstream or downstream. Like many of my friends, I am convinced my life is ruled by Sod's Law! So in this situation, I can virtually guarantee that I will choose to walk in the wrong direction and then have to retrace my steps. The simple solution is that by deliberately aiming to one side of the junction by an amount that is consistent with any error I feel I might make, I have a far better chance of choosing the right direction (see Figure 32).

When using this technique, I usually aim off by a distance equivalent to about 10% of the distance to be walked. For example, if the stream junction is 400 metres away, I calculate my bearing to take me 50 metres to one side of it. Under normal circumstances, it is better to head towards the upstream side of a stream junction so that you then walk downhill to get to your objective. However, you need to consider a number of other factors before deciding to which side you are going to head. These will include such things as the nature of the terrain to either side of your objective, and the direction of your subsequent route.

It is also worth bearing in mind that the more acute your angle of approach to a linear feature, the more error you are likely to make in terms of your position along the feature. This means that route 2 in Figure 32 is a poor alternative on two counts!

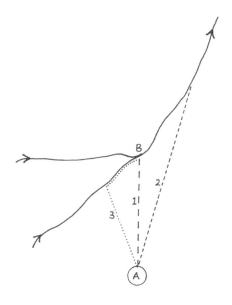

Making life difficult – resections

It would be remiss of me not to make mention of **resections**, even though – for reasons that I hope will soon become abundantly clear – I consider them to be about as useful and convenient as chocolate sunhats!

Let us assume that you are back in the middle of the gently undulating section of heather moorland with only a rough idea of where you are. The visibility is reasonable, however, and as you can see an obvious feature in the distance that you can positively identify on the map, you use your compass to take a magnetic bearing as described Chapter 11. After converting this to a grid bearing, you place your compass on the map in such a way that the orienting arrow points to the top of the map, the orienting lines run parallel to the north-south grid lines, and one side of the base plate (or one of the lines in the base plate) touches the feature on which you sighted. What you have effectively done is narrowed down your possible position to a thin line, for you must be standing somewhere along the edge of the base plate (or line in the base plate) that touches the feature on which you sighted. This process is precisely the same as that described to above when locating yourself on a linear feature, except that in this example you are not standing on a linear feature.

In order to do a classic resection, you should use one side of the base plate rather than one of the lines in the base plate, because the next stage is to draw a line along the side of the base plate to indicate, on the map, the line along which you know you must be standing. Once you have drawn this line, take a second bearing on another recognisable feature, preferably about 120° away from the first. Treat this bearing in exactly the same way as the first, and draw a second line on the map. This second line will cross the first, and the point at which the two lines cross will be your position, its accuracy depending upon the precision of your compass work. If you wish to be even more accurate, take a third bearing, preferably a further 120° away, and then draw a third line. Because of slight inaccuracies, the three lines will not meet at a precise point, but you will end up with a small triangle. Your position will most likely be somewhere inside that triangle (although it could be slightly outside it, depending upon how accurate you have been!) (see Figure 33).

I have several problems with resections, not the least of which is that if the visibility is good enough for you to see three features at roughly 120° intervals, you really should be able to work out your position by map interpretation alone, especially if you set your map and use line of sight (as described in Chapter 7). Resections are also time consuming, and ninety-nine times out of a hundred, there will almost certainly be an easier way of working out your position!

Figure 33 | *Classic resection.*

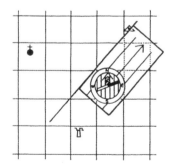
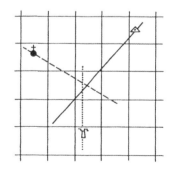

Useful information – aspect of slope

Measuring the direction that a slope faces involves a simple technique which can give you extremely useful information, especially if you are near a saddle or col, or the head of a valley. Indeed, the technique can even be used to pinpoint your position when, for example, walking around the top of a curving Scottish corrie, or in other places where the direction of slope changes constantly as you walk, or is unique in the area in which you are standing.

Photo 31 | *The aspect of slope is different in virtually every part of this photo, and the snow has picked out the watercourses and gullies which, in the main, correspond to the fall lines.*

The basic idea is to face directly down slope along the **fall line** (the general direction in which a ball would roll if dropped), then point the DOT arrow directly away from you in such a way that it lies along the fall line, at 90° to the line of the slope (at right angles to the contour lines). Take a magnetic bearing in

the normal way, convert it to a grid bearing, and then place the compass on the map with the orienting arrow pointing towards the top of the map and the orienting lines parallel to the north-south grid lines. Your position will be where the contour lines run parallel to the end of the base plate. This is obviously more accurate and easier to see in some areas than in others (see Figure 34).

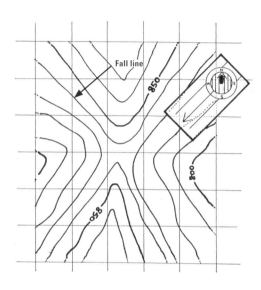

Figure 34 | *Using aspect of slope in a col or saddle. The aspect of slope changes depending on your position relative to the saddle. Having measured the aspect as described above, in this example your position must be somewhere in the top left-hand quadrant of the figure – the only place where the DOT arrow points straight down the fall line (shown in red) and the descending contour lines run parallel to the end of the base plate.*

Like most compass techniques, this can also be used in reverse, taking the information from the map and then using it on the ground. This is useful when, for example, you are traversing around the head of a valley and wish to strike off at a particular point. Place your compass on the map with the DOT arrow pointing directly down the slope and one of the lines in the base plate touching the position where you wish to strike off, and at right angles to the contour lines at that point. Take a grid bearing and convert it to a magnetic bearing. Now walk along the top of the slope pointing the DOT arrow directly downhill (at right angles to the slope), and continue until the red end of the needle lies directly over the orienting arrow. When this happens, you will be standing at the position from which you wish to leave the edge (see Figure 35). There are numerous other applications, such as checking that you are about to use the right descent gully, etc.

Having explained the technique, I must point out that, as with the resection technique described above, and particularly if the visibility is reasonable, it is often easier and quicker to use aspect of slope simply by setting your map and using line of sight.

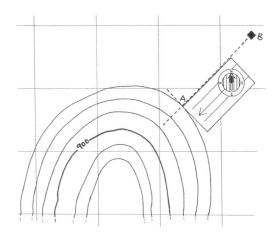

Figure 35 │ *Using aspect of slope to pinpoint where to leave the head of a valley.*

Using physical waypoints

I will use the term 'waypoint' in another context when I come to discuss the use (and abuse) of GPS devices in Chapter 18. In this context, however, I am using the term to refer to any feature which is easily recognisable both on the map and on the ground, and which is readily visible over a reasonably long distance. As such I am describing a **physical waypoint** rather than a **virtual waypoint**. Such features can be invaluable in navigation as they give the eye something on which to focus. If you can see something on the ground and also know where it is on the map, you can use it not only to get a sense of direction and distance, but you can also set your map using it, you can use it when using line of sight techniques, and you can even take a magnetic bearing on it in order to help you relocate yourself.

Photo 32 │ *The flat-topped summit on the ridge is a good example of a physical waypoint – visible from miles around and instantly recognisable. I also know the location of the large tree – useful on days when the visibility is not so good.*

Whenever you are out walking, try to find a physical waypoint early in the day. Particularly when walking in an area that you do not know well, choose these physical waypoints from the ground rather than from the map, because they must be features that you can recognise instantly. I cannot tell you the type of feature to use – only you can decide what you find instantly recognisable! If you are using a laminated map or map extract, mark the position of your chosen waypoint using a Chinagraph pencil.

On a good day's walk, the physical waypoint that started in front of you may eventually disappear behind, or the waypoint that was once instantly recognisable may change shape and merge with the background. It will therefore often be necessary to choose a succession of different physical waypoints as the day progresses. Indeed, if you can identify two waypoints at an acute angle to one another, you can use them to work out your approximate location very quickly using line of sight (without there being any need to consult your compass), after which you can fine-tune your position using map interpretation.

Dominant feet

In the same way that almost all of us are right- or left-handed, most people are either right- or left-footed – in other words, most of us have a dominant foot. In some people, this can be a major influence, and can affect their ability to walk in a straight line. To find out how much your dominant foot influences you, find a football or rugby field, stand between the goal posts at one end of the pitch, then close your eyes and take fifty or so paces towards the goal at the far end. When you open your eyes, if you are left foot dominant, the goal will be to your left; if you are right foot dominant, the goal will be to your right. This is simply because your dominant foot takes a slightly stronger stride.

Whilst this is usually not too much of a problem, the effect can be remarkably strong in some people, causing them to veer off to one side even when following a compass bearing. If, for example, someone is strongly left foot dominant, they will tend to stand to the right of a spot when spotting (or to the right of the person when leapfrogging), with their left foot near the spot or person. This means they are already a metre or so off course. If you are following a bearing of 500 metres in visibility of 20 metres, this single factor can put you 25 metres or more off course by the time you get near your objective – which means you will not be able to see it!

Another situation in which this can have a significant effect is when you are trying to walk in a more or less straight line, perhaps heading in a rough direction in order to reach a long, linear feature. Particularly in relatively featureless terrain such as moorland, it is very easy to become disorientated, and unless you keep checking your compass, you can easily veer off course and head in the wrong direction without noticing. This can also occur if there is no definite horizon, as can happen in misty or snowy conditions, and in dense woodland. There are, for example, documented examples from the Amazon rainforest, where people have survived a plane crash, and realising that the wreckage cannot be seen through the canopy, have tried to walk out to get help without a compass, only to walk in a complete circle and arrive back at the crash site a day or so later.

To recap

Bearings are simply invisible straight lines, so their use is limited solely by your imagination. If you can draw a line on the map, you can follow it on the ground – if you can measure a line on the ground, you can draw it on a map.

Using a combination of invisible lines (bearings) and physical lines (linear features) can simplify your navigation tremendously.

You can use your compass to give you useful information about which way a slope faces at a particular point, and like most compass techniques, this can be done both from map to ground, and from ground to map.

It is also useful to use recognisable features as physical way-points in order to give the eye something on which to focus.

Be aware that some people have a dominant foot which can cause them to veer off course, particularly in featureless terrain or situations where there is no definite horizon.

16 ATTACK POINTS AND HANDRAILS

There will undoubtedly come a time when the feature for which you are heading lies in a difficult or awkward position. It may even be impossible to reach safely along a direct route from your present position owing to some obstacle lying across your path. When this happens, you may be able to get around the problem by aiming off, as described earlier, but you will find this well-nigh impossible if your destination does not lie on or extremely close to a linear feature. You might also consider using a dog-leg bearing, but this, too, may not be the most convenient option.

A possible alternative is to approach your objective via an **attack point**. This is quite simply a different point that lies fairly close to your destination and which you can reach with relative ease. From this attack point, you then use a combination of bearing and pacing in order to reach your target far more simply than if you were to head straight for it. In many ways, the use of attack points is an extension of the route-planning and route-finding skills discussed in Chapter 19.

Referring to Figure 36, let us assume that you are standing at the trig point (A) in conditions of decreasing visibility, and you wish to get to the bothy (B). You cannot use the direct route because of the crag lying directly across your path, and making a detour using either a box bearing or a dog-leg would be a lengthy and unnecessarily complicated procedure. Happily, there is a far better alternative available that makes use of an attack point.

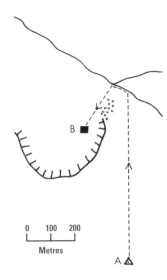

B ■

0   100   200
Metres

A ⧌

Figure 36 | *Using an attack point.*

You first need to choose a suitable attack point. In an ideal world, this should be as close to your destination as possible, and certainly within 500 metres as an absolute maximum. It should also be relatively simple to find, and instantly recognisable. In our example, the stream junction fits the bill perfectly. Work out the grid bearing from your present position to the attack point, and convert it to a magnetic bearing in the usual way. Because, in this example, the attack point lies on a linear feature (the stream), this is another situation where aiming off will be useful, simply because if you followed a direct bearing and reached the stream with the junction nowhere in sight, you would not know whether to walk to the left or right. It also allows you to keep well away from the edge of the cliff. Having reached the stream and found the junction, you then use your map to calculate a further bearing from the junction to the bothy, measuring the distance so that you can gauge your progress via pacing. Note how, in this example, we are using a number of different techniques in combination with one another. This, to my mind, is the real art of navigation – knowing when to use which combination of features to manage any given situation.

If, whilst following your bearing to the attack point, the visibility improves and you catch a glimpse of the bothy, there is no reason why you should not head straight for it, so long as you are certain that you are well past the dangerous ground where the crag curves around. If you do decide that it is safe for you to leave your bearing and head straight to the now visible bothy, it would be wise to use your compass to take a magnetic bearing on the bothy, and to stay as close to this bearing as possible. In this way, if the visibility closes in again, you can follow this new bearing to the bothy. If you are forced to detour by the rocky ground, keep your eyes on the weather and, if it looks as though the visibility is going to close in again, check that your bearing to the bothy is still correct. If it is not, either correct it by taking another magnetic bearing, or head directly towards the stream, make your way to your original attack point and reach the bothy from there.

One of the easiest and most effective methods of navigating in mountain and moorland areas is to use **handrails**. Indeed, the real trick to keeping your poor visibility navigation simple and effective is to choose suitable handrails whenever possible. A handrail is simply a well-defined linear feature such as a path or track, field boundary, stream, edge of forest, narrow valley, sharp ridge, or break of slope. Even contour lines can be used as handrails, but see the comments about traversing and following contours in Chapter 20. Consider also that, contrary to popular belief, there is nothing wrong with you heading towards the top of a cliff in misty conditions – *as long as you know it is there!* It is a natural handrail and can be used to aid navigation. However, you should always be extremely wary about using the tops of cliffs as handrails if you are unsure of your position, and should not use them in winter conditions when they may be corniced.

Photo 34 | *There are a number of handrails in this photo: the narrow valley to the left; the break of slope ahead; and the path crossing from mid right towards top left.*

A compass bearing is actually a type of handrail, but owing to the fact that it is invisible, it takes a certain amount of concentration to follow it. It is far easier to use natural, visible handrails whenever they are available. No matter what the conditions, handrails can be a great aid to map interpretation, and even in the poorest visibility, they can offer a means of quickly and easily getting from one position to another without having to spend all your time with your nose in a map or following compass bearings.

Referring to Figure 37, let us assume that you are standing by the cairn at point A, and you want to get to the stream junction at point B. There is, of course, nothing to stop you taking a bearing on the junction itself, or, better still, aiming off to the upstream side of the junction. Calculating and then following this bearing will not take an inordinate amount of time and effort, but in this particular situation, there is an easier option using handrails. The simplest way to reach the stream junction is to head in a general northerly direction until you reach the forest, then turn right and follow the edge of the wood until you reach the corner. Once there, continue in roughly the same direction until you reach the stream (or, if the visibility is awful, turn left and follow the edge of the wood to reach the stream), then follow this down to the junction. You have only had to consult your compass once, and then very briefly, in order to give you a general direction right at the start.

Probably the most important point to realise is that navigating in mountain and moorland terrain in poor visibility has nothing to do with heroics. The real art lies in making life easy for yourself.

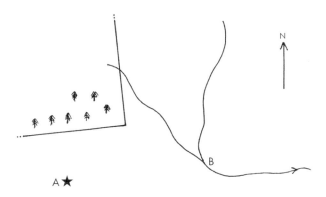

Figure 37 | *Using handrails to make life easy.*

To recap

Particularly in poor visibility, making use of attack points and handrails whenever possible will make your life much easier.

Attack points are used when your destination is difficult to reach directly from your current location. The basic idea is to detour to the attack point, and then reach your destination from there. Good attack points will be relatively simple to find, easy to recognise, and close to your objective.

Handrails are well defined linear features that can be easily reached and then followed without there being any need for you to refer constantly to your map or compass. It is often possible to link several linear features together in such a way that you can reach your destination easily, without having to refer to your map and compass with monotonous regularity.

17 IMPROVISED DIRECTION FINDING

Navigation is all about being observant and using as much of the information around you as possible to help you build your picture of the ground. It would therefore be remiss of me not to give at least a passing mention to the wealth of folklore and countryside 'laws' that can be used to help you get an idea of direction. Some are amazingly reliable, whereas others need to be treated with a degree of caution!

For example, because the sun is always slightly to the south in the British Isles and particularly so in winter, any atmospheric icing or lying snow tends to thaw faster on the sunnier south-facing slopes and last longer on the more shadowy north-facing slopes. However, that is not the whole story. You also need to take into consideration that because the air is usually warmer in the afternoon than in the morning, more melting takes place in the afternoon (when the sun is shining on west facing slopes) than in the morning (when it is shining on east facing slopes). Thus, slopes facing south-west will often lose their snow first, and those facing north-east, last. It would be good if it was that simple, but there is still more to consider, because you also need to be aware that the wind direction can have a significant effect. If, for example, there was heavy snowfall driven by a north-easterly wind, more snow will be deposited on the south-west facing slopes than on the north-east facing slopes, simply because snow tends to build up on lee slopes. This means that even though more melting takes place on the south-westerly slopes, the greater depth of snow may cause it to remain there for longer. This method of gauging direction is therefore not very reliable!

There are plenty of other examples, but many are less than reliable. For example, it is commonly believed that (in the northern hemisphere) shade-loving plants such as ferns, mosses and lichens always grow more profusely on the shadier, northern side of a tree/boulder/wall. However, this is not strictly true, for although some such plants thrive in the shade, most plants (including many mosses) tend to have their most lush growth on the side of the tree/boulder/wall facing the sun. In any event, almost all plants tend to grow towards the sun, so their flowers and most prolific growth is likely to be towards the south.

The wind can also be used to give a sense of direction, as long as you are observant. For example, if you have been travelling with the wind on your left cheek and you suddenly realise that it is now in your face, you should question whether it is the wind or you who have changed direction! You should also consider that, because the prevailing winds in Britain tend to come from the south-west, many isolated and exposed trees will be bent towards the north-east. Be aware, however, that mountains make their own weather, and local topography can have a significant effect on wind direction. For example, steep-sided valleys can funnel the wind and change its direction, meaning that the wind may be blowing in different directions on either side of a hill.

Whilst the examples above show that some of the folklore should be treated with caution, getting an idea of direction from the sun and the stars is far more reliable. In all the techniques outlined below, I have assumed that you are in the northern hemisphere.

Stellar navigation

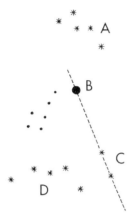

Figure 38 | *The Pole Star: A = Cassiopeia (shaped like a flat M or W), B = Pole Star, C = Pointers, D = The Plough.*

You can find north without the use of a compass on a clear night by looking at the stars. You need to find Polaris (also known as the Pole Star or the North Star), which is always to the north, and around which all other stars will appear to rotate. The easiest way to find this star is by reference to The Plough – a constellation which most people can recognise (see Figure 38). The position of the Pole Star is indicated by the **pointers**, and the Pole Star itself is about four times further away than the distance between the pointers. Do not make the common mistake of thinking that the Pole Star is one of the brightest stars in the sky – it is actually quite dim!

Whilst on the subject of stellar navigation, it is also possible to use lunar navigation and get a sense of direction from the moon. If the moon rises before sunset, the illuminated side will be to the west. If, however, the moon rises after midnight, the illuminated side will be to the east.

Solar navigation

On a reasonably sunny day, you can easily get a sense of direction without the aid of a compass by using a watch – as long as it shows the correct time in GMT, without any adjustment having been made for daylight saving. Holding the watch flat and ignoring the minute hand, point the hour hand directly at the sun. South will then be half-way between the hour hand and 12 o'clock. You can also do this if you have a digital watch – simply draw a picture of a clock face showing the right time, and use this instead!

If the sun is casting a shadow, you can also get a good idea of direction using a stick or walking pole, although this does take a little time. Place the stick upright on a stretch of level ground, and mark the tip of the shadow it casts. Now wait for at least a quarter of an hour (by which time the shadow will have moved), and mark the new position of the tip of the shadow. If you now draw a line between the two points, this line will align west-east, with the first mark to the west. If you now stand immediately in front of the stick with the first mark to your left and the second to your right, you will be facing north.

Figure 39 | Direction finding via the sun and shadows.

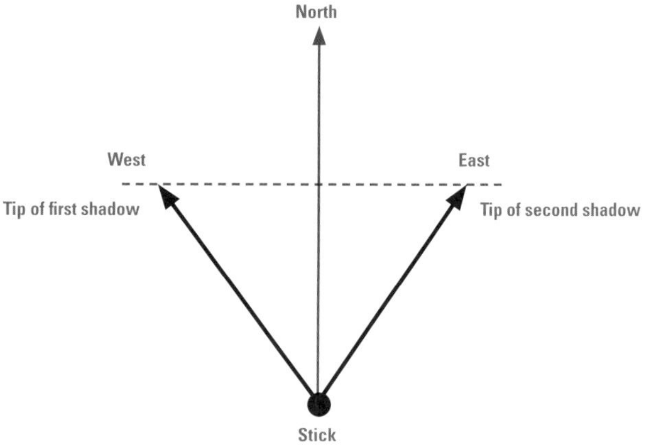

To recap

There are several ways by which you can get a rough sense of direction without having to refer to your compass. Some of the more obscure folklore methods are of dubious reliability, but you can use such things as the stars, the moon, and the sun with confidence.

18 USING AND ABUSING GPS

I am on record as being a staunch critic of GPS devices. However, I am happy to concede that I have changed my mind somewhat, mainly because the technology has developed, and I now believe that these devices can play a useful role when it comes to mountain and moorland navigation. Having said this, I also believe that they are often misused, and that their role in this type of navigation is largely misunderstood and often overplayed. Perhaps the biggest, single danger is that they encourage an over-reliance on gadgetry at the expense of good map interpretation and basic navigation skills. Additionally, as we will see, if you rely predominantly on a GPS device, you run the danger of becoming a slave either to straight-line navigation, or to a predetermined, down-loaded route, neither of which are the best way to travel.

The biggest advantage of the GPS system is that it can give the user easy access to information which can be of help when navigating in poor visibility or across featureless terrain, and which otherwise would be difficult or time-consuming to obtain. Conversely, the biggest disadvantage is that it is easy to be beguiled by the technology and to see a GPS device as a substitute for good map interpretation and conventional, mechanical compass techniques, which it demonstrably is not. In fact, despite the advances that have been made, GPS devices are still neither as consistently accurate nor as reliable as standard navigation techniques, and should never be used as a stand-alone navigation tool. For a start, they need a clear view of the sky if they are to be precise, and they are therefore less than reliable in steep-sided valleys or thick forest, even with the latest high-sensitivity antennae. They also stop working when the batteries go flat, which is still a monotonously common problem, for despite advances, they drain batteries at an alarming rate, particularly in cold, winter conditions. Moreover, carrying spare batteries is not as straightforward an answer as it may appear, as anyone who has had to open the battery compartment of a GPS device in even mildly wet conditions will confirm.

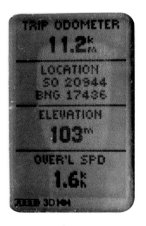

TRIP ODOMETER
11.2ᵏ
LOCATION
SO 20944
BNG 17436
ELEVATION
103ᵐ
OVER'L SPD
1.6ᵏ
3D

Photo 36 | *Trip page of a*
GPS device.

Historically, much of the criticism levelled at GPS devices resulted from the fact that the satellite system on which they work is largely controlled by the US military, who until comparatively recently broadcast deliberately inaccurate information to the civilian population. This **selective availability** (or SA) only allowed positioning to within 100 metres for 95% of the time. However, SA has now been removed, and the result is a system that is accurate to within 20 metres (often less) for 95% of the time. Whilst this is true of horizontal positioning, the same cannot be said of vertical positioning, simply because the GPS compass can only use satellites that are above the horizon. This means that the accuracy of vertical information is not as accurate – typically to within about 50 metres for 95% of the time.

In the most basic terms, a GPS device is simply a small, computerised satellite receiver with a screen, and different makes and models will obviously offer slightly different features. However, most allow you to display a number of page options on the screen, and these usually include:

A **satellite page** – which shows you how many satellites are being used together with an estimate of the likely accuracy of the device;

A **map page** – which shows you where you are relative to a map, the detail of which will vary according to the model of GPS device you are using;

A **navigation page** – which gives you information such as your heading, speed, and how far you are from your destination; and

A **trip page** – which usually gives you the option to display several of a large number of fields including position, altitude, average speed, distance covered, etc.

There is also usually a **menu page** – which allows you to access a number of other useful functions such as waypoint marking and retrieval, track back functions, stored routes, etc.

No matter what the make or model, you must ensure that the device is set up correctly. Two important options that need to be set are the map datum (so that you can use it with British maps) and position format (so that positions are given as grid references rather than in terms of latitude and longitude). You also need to set the device to use metric units of measurement as opposed to imperial, to work on Greenwich Mean Time (and automatically adjust for day-light saving time), and to take account of the local magnetic variation when showing bearings.

I would hazard a guess that many experienced hillwalkers who own a GPS device leave it in the bottom of their rucksack and only get it out when they are uncertain of their position and need to confirm it. Yet a good GPS device can give you a wealth of other useful (and useless!) information. In addition to giving you your position (usually as a ten-figure grid reference), the **trip computer** can tell you such things as your maximum and average speed, and the distance you have covered either in total or on any leg of navigation. Another useful feature is the **track** function. This can be used in several ways, two of the more helpful being **track log** and **track back**. In broad terms, a **track log** is where the GPS device remembers your precise route, displaying this on the map page and storing the information in its memory. **Track back** then reads this information and displays it in such a way that you can retrace your steps, very accurately, and with a minimum of mental effort. Additionally, many models allow you to download the track log information to your computer when you return home, which means you can not only store the route for future reference, but also display it graphically on a digital map.

Photo 37 | *A GPS device can give you useful information that otherwise would be difficult to obtain ... particularly in conditions such as these.*

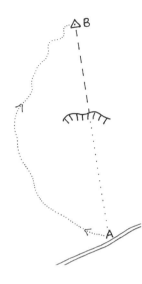

Figure 40 | Abusing GPS 1.
A straight-line (GPS) course
from B to A will take you
over the top of the cliff!

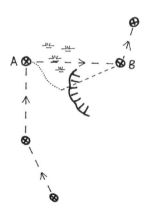

Figure 41 | Abusing GPS 2.
For explanation, see opposite.

You can also input grid references yourself and ask the device to take you to the positions to which they refer, in which case many models will give you an estimate of how long it will take you to get there, and how far away you are. These inputted grid references are known as **waypoints**, and in this instance they do not have to be highly visible features such as the physical waypoints I described in Chapter 15. Instead, they are simply positions that are stored in the GPS device's memory either by inputting a grid reference from a map, or by storing a visited location by the simple push of a button.

The display will also show you in which direction you should walk in order to reach any chosen waypoint, but herein lies one of the dangers, for a GPS device can only work in straight lines between known waypoints. The arrow on the display will always point directly to the waypoint for which you are heading, but it will not warn you if there is a hidden cliff lying across your path! One of the biggest abuses of GPS devices, therefore, is when people store where they left their car as a waypoint, and later in the day ask the GPS device to navigate back to the car (see Figure 40). Similar abuse occurs when people input the grid reference of a destination (say, a bothy), and get the GPS device to navigate them there without any reference to their map.

One way to avoid this problem is to use **multiple waypoints**. I know of people who will sit down the night before a walk and input literally dozens of waypoints into a GPS device so that they can follow the route the next day. Their argument is that the more waypoints they input, the safer will be their route, and the less likely they will be to suffer from the disadvantages of straight-line navigation. From my point of view, whilst multiple waypoints alleviate some of the problems of straight-line navigation, it does not solve them, as a quick glance at Figure 41 will show. Because the GPS display arrow always points straight to the next waypoint, any deviation from the straight line route occasioned by, say, a very boggy area, will result in a new heading that could lead you into dangerous ground. It is, of course, now possible to download routes from the internet, but whilst this might reduce the problems mentioned above (depending, of course, on the quality of the download and the number of waypoints used), people who lace up the route like this become slaves to their navigation. It is the GPS device that controls where they walk, not their desire to see what lies over the next horizon.

If you wish to input location data before going on a walk, or to get your GPS device to take you to a predetermined point which you have not yet visited, you will need to tell it exactly where you want to go. This can be done in a number of ways. Firstly, if you wish to input information about a complete walk, you can connect your GPS device to your computer and download the information from one of the many GPS-enabled walking sites on the internet. You can also do this by hand, tracing the route on a map, accurately calculating the grid references of loads of waypoints, and then inputting these into your GPS device. The latter method is useful because it can be done during a walk, allowing you, for example, to get your GPS device to direct you to a nearby bothy – so long as you know there is nothing that could be hazardous lying across your route. This is another situation in which a romer scale can be indispensable, as it allows you to measure grid references with a high degree of accuracy (see Figure 42). Place your romer scale on the map with the top right-hand corner of the appropriate scale touching the feature you wish to locate. In this position, it is a simple matter to read off a grid reference which is accurate to eight figures.

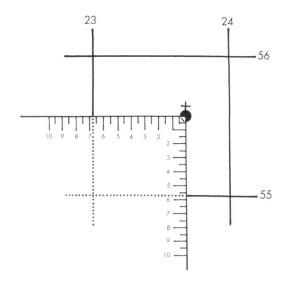

Figure 42 | *Using a romer to calculate grid references. The eight-figure grid ref. of the church is 23675556.*

The more advanced map-enabled GPS devices display large scale (up to 1:25,000) digital mapping in full colour. Many allow you to enlarge the map and place a pin onto a precise location, thus making it unnecessary to input the grid reference. These models also display your position as a small dot or arrow on the digital map. This point remains stationary in the centre of the screen, and the map scrolls as you move. Although this is useful as it gives you information about your immediate surroundings, it is often only a snapshot of the area as the size of the map is limited by the size of the display screen.

The development of navigation apps that can be used on GPS enabled smart phones and tablets has great potential. There are, for example, several free apps which display your position – usually as a six-, eight-, or even ten-figure grid reference. Because these apps use the GPS system, they do not require a mobile network or Wi-Fi signal to work, and the GPS receiver on the phone can be set to turn on only when the app is in use, thus minimising battery drain. Additionally, the Ordnance Survey now offers a free digital download with each paper Explorer map purchased, and this can be used in conjunction with a free OS Maps app, which has many of the features associated with dedicated GPS devices. As useful as these apps are, however, they currently suffer from the same disadvantages as the dedicated GPS devices, especially those associated with battery life. There is also the problem of the weather, because whilst most GPS devices designed for walkers are rugged and weatherproof, the same cannot be said of many modern smart phones, and whilst waterproof and shockproof cases are available for most models of smart phone, some of these affect the functionality of the touch screen, which is not helpful.

Technological advances continue apace, and I am certain that GPS devices will increasingly be able to store more and more complex digital mapping data, allowing them to display accurate and useful information in conjunction with detailed, scrolling maps that indicate your current position. I am also certain that we will see increasing numbers of models containing some form of beacon that will allow their location to be pinpointed, perhaps even after the main batteries have failed. Indeed, this technology is already with us, as anyone who has used the 'Find my device' app will confirm.

All things considered, GPS is undoubtedly one of the most important developments in terrestrial navigation for centuries. However, I firmly believe that, so far as mountain and moorland navigation is concerned, it is not a substitute for good map interpretation and more conventional poor visibility techniques.

You can navigate safely without a GPS device – but you cannot navigate safely without a map and a conventional compass.

To recap

GPS devices are now far more accurate than was once the case, but they still have several disadvantages, not the least of which is that they can only work in straight lines when following a route. They can give the user additional information which can be of help when navigating in poor visibility or across featureless terrain, but they should not be seen as stand-alone devices, nor as a substitute for map interpretation or more conventional compass techniques.

19 ROUTE SELECTION

Planning your walk and then selecting the best route is an important part of the greater art of navigation, and whilst, like so many other aspects, it is best learned through experience, a few thoughts on the subject will not go amiss. By way of explanation and for the purposes of clarity, I am going to make a distinction between **route planning** (working out where the overall walk will go) and **route finding** (deciding on the precise route to follow between specific points on the walk). In some ways this distinction is arbitrary, for in practice the two tend to merge.

Route planning

I am often asked how one should go about planning a walk. This is an impossible question to answer, because different people have different expectations and requirements. Some people are looking to get their enjoyment from the sheer physical effort of a long, strenuous mountain day, whereas others prefer the short, sharp shock of a technical scramble, or a relatively gentle stroll with great views. The combinations are infinite. Having said this, whatever the preferences, there are a number of things that should be considered before making a final choice.

Route planning is the general process of deciding roughly where to go on a walk (the overall plan). At one extreme, particularly when you are walking in an area you do not know particularly well, this basic route planning might involve a lengthy and detailed study of the map, possibly in conjunction with a guide book. At the other extreme, when walking in more familiar surroundings, it may involve little more than a quick glance at the weather forecast and a chat with your walking companions.

Photo 39 | *When planning your route, think about the nature of the terrain you will be crossing.*

Whatever the scenario, when doing this basic route planning you should think about such things as the size, fitness and experience of the party, the type of terrain to be crossed, the time of year (and thus the amount of daylight available), and whether you intend to camp overnight as part of the walk (and will, therefore, be carrying more weight). Once you have decided on an outline route, Naismith's Rule (see Chapter 13) will give you a reasonable idea of how long it will take, but do not forget to adjust this timing to take account of the factors mentioned above. You should also take note of the local weather forecast, and for this reason it is arguably better not to make any definite plans until the night before you are due to go. Leaving it this late has the added advantage that everything will be fresh in your mind, because as you study the map in order to work out your outline route, you will also begin to get a mental picture of the general topography of the area.

Whilst studying your map, try to picture the basic shape of the region by concentrating first on the contour patterns. Think about such things as the steepness and shape of the slopes and the location of the larger ridges and valleys. Look then for the major linear features, particularly those that can be used as handrails, and think about ways of escaping from the walk if things go wrong. What you are doing is using the layer system (see Chapter 5) to build up your picture of the ground piece by piece. After linear features come the pinpoint symbols – in this instance look for features that will be useful either for micro-navigation or as highly visible waypoints – and then look at the area symbols to get an idea of the likely conditions underfoot. Large areas of boggy ground or extensive boulder fields can be very trying, as can attempting to force your way through closely planted conifers. What you are trying to do is build up as accurate a picture of the ground as you can. Not only will this enable you to plan your walk more effectively, but also the background knowledge thus obtained will be extremely useful if something unexpected happens and you need to alter your plans.

Route finding

Whilst route planning is a general, outline process, route finding is far more detailed, being concerned with the precise route of each stage (or leg) of the walk. There is an art to selecting the easiest, or most suitable, route between two points – it is a continuous process that starts from the moment you leave the car, and ends only when you have returned at the end of the day.

Photo 40 | *The quickest route is not always a straight line. It is almost always better and quickest to zigzag on steep terrain.*

A fairly common misconception held by those new to walking is that the quickest route is always a straight line. This is rarely the case, as witnessed by the fact that most good paths follow the lie of the land rather than travel in a dead straight line. Similarly, the easiest route is rarely the shortest. Indeed, it is often possible to tell the experience of a group of walkers simply by watching the route they follow. Inexperienced parties will often walk directly from one point to another, perhaps even toiling up one side of a short, steep spur only to drop down on the other side. A more experienced party is more likely to walk around the base of the spur, or take a gently rising traverse line, instead of tackling it direct. One of the few rules of mountaincraft is that you should try to avoid losing or gaining height unnecessarily. It is a waste of both time and effort to climb 100 metres only to lose it again when there is a far easier, albeit slightly longer, alternative – unless, of course, you are heading for a particularly spectacular viewpoint! (See also Chapter 20 and Figure 46.)

Particularly when walking in unfamiliar areas in poor visibility, be aware of the danger of descending **convex slopes**. Convex slopes are those that become steeper as they descend, and owing to their shape, it is impossible to see what is below you. Obviously, you should see any sizeable cliff from your map (assuming you know where you are), but drops of less than about five metres may not be shown – and five metres is a long way to fall! In any case, the psychology of height will play an important role. Most people can stand on a tea tray on one leg and hop up and down, but put that tea tray on a pedestal two metres high and few people can do it. Despite the fact that you are physically able, your brain will not let you. The same thing can happen when descending convex slopes. Everything is okay until you break through the mist and find a steepening, muddy slope below you. At this point your brain may decide not to let you move up or down!

It is generally far safer to descend **concave slopes** (those that become less steep as you descend). Although you may have difficulties on the steep part at the top, you can always see what is coming up and know that the slope is lessening. If your understanding of contour patterns is good, you should recognise that convex slopes are shown by contour lines that become closer together as they lose height, whereas concave slopes are shown by contour lines that become closer together as they gain height. This was illustrated earlier in the book in Figure 7.

It is also advisable to avoid using gullies or stream beds as descent routes. Although they may represent tempting handrails, your view of the surrounding countryside is likely to be very restricted, and they are usually full of loose, slippery rocks. Don't forget, too, that water always takes the line of least resistance – for example it likes to travel vertically downwards whenever it can! Even if you do not fall over the edge of a waterfall, you may be faced with a vertical drop or an impassable section, and it may be impossible to climb out of the gully without retracing your steps for some distance. If you have had any difficulty on the way down, you can be certain you will have even more difficulty on the way back up.

Photo 41 | *Stream beds do not always make the best descent routes.*

Finally, when selecting your route, be aware that your eyes can lie. In broad terms, when you look uphill your eyes tend to foreshorten the distance, whilst when you look downhill they tend to elongate it. Additionally, the further away you look, the flatter the landscape appears. These phenomena are discussed in more detail in Chapter 23.

Route cards

Although it might sound tedious, it makes perfect sense to draw up some form of route card before setting off into the wild blue yonder. This can be used in a number of ways, not only as an aid to safety, but also as a helpful reference document in those situations where, owing to worsening weather conditions or some other problem, you have a lot on your mind apart from the navigation.

In its simplest form, a route card consists of a brief outline of your proposed route, together with perhaps a few details of the places you are going to visit or pass along the way, and maybe a rough description of a couple of potential escape routes. A more detailed route card will contain grid references, compass bearings, distances, estimated times, escape routes, specific comments or warnings about potential hazards, and a host of other information about the party and the equipment carried which you feel may be useful.

Route cards come in a multitude of different formats, and there are no hard and fast rules regarding how they should be laid out. However, whatever your preferred format, it is essential that the information on the card is clear both to you and to others, with no ambiguities. The importance of clarity should not be underestimated, because the route card is not only there to help you, but also to help others find you should you get into difficulties. Before you set off on your walk, you should make two copies of the card, and leave one with someone responsible, together with a note of the time by which you expect to return. Do not place the copy on the parcel shelf of your car, nor under the windscreen wiper – you are simply telling potential thieves how long they have got! In the event that you do not return by the stated time, the information on the card will be of help to anyone looking for you (e.g. mountain rescue).

Unfortunately, route cards are shunned by some walkers, because they believe that by using them they deny themselves the freedom to roam, this being the main reason they went walking in the first place. Whilst I would be the last person to insist that everyone should rigidly follow a route card description each time they go walking, I feel sure that most people would agree that you should always leave at least a few details of your approximate route with a responsible person, even if you have had a lot of experience. After all, even experienced people can have accidents. However, if you do leave details of your route with someone, it is vital you let them know when you return. There have been countless occasions when a mountain rescue team has been needlessly called out to look for an overdue party, only to find that they have descended safely and are enjoying themselves in the local pub, having forgotten to tell anyone that they are back. As you can imagine, rescue team members are less than impressed when this happens!

Photo 42 | *Route cards can be very useful when your hands are fumbling and your brain is frozen.*

Writing a route card has other advantages that can make a big difference to a day's walking, especially if you are in an unfamiliar area. For a start, in order to compile one with any measure of accuracy, you will need to sit down and study your map before you go, thereby getting to know the basic shape of the area. In the process, it is a good idea to look for one or more **escape routes** along which you can easily retreat, should the need arise. These should be easy-to-follow, straightforward routes leading down into the nearest valley or civilisation. Do not make the mistake of thinking that the easiest route will be the quickest or the most direct – a good escape route is one along which it is relatively simple to navigate, which gives you as much shelter as possible from inclement conditions, and down which it is possible to assist a slightly injured person. Knowledge of the terrain plays an important role, so if you are less than about a third of the way through your walk, you will probably find it easiest to retrace your steps. Similarly, if you are more than about two-thirds of the way through your walk, it is probably just as easy to keep going.

Textbook escape routes occur very rarely in practice. Whatever routes you decide upon, choose them with care and in the knowledge that if you are forced to use them, something will have gone wrong. You could well be tired, wet and cold, and trying to help an injured person. At the very least, outline details of your escape routes should be given on *both* copies of your route card so that, if the worst comes to the worst, any rescue team will know where to look in addition to your main route.

Another advantage of route cards is that they allow you to calculate and note down accurate compass bearings and time and distance estimations in comfort, before going onto the hill. It can be extremely difficult to work out a compass bearing when your hands are cold and fumbling, the rain is lashing into your eyes, and your map has a life of its own owing to gusts of wind, yet this is the very time when you might need an accurate bearing! Your route card, carefully worked out the night before, can solve this problem.

Furthermore, you should not feel compelled to follow your route card religiously. The greatest strength of any route card is that it gives you the basic skeleton of your walk, and tells potential rescuers about the places you are planning to visit and the type of walking you are planning to do. Chances are that if you do not come back, you are off route anyway! However, if something unforeseen does occur, even if you have deliberately wandered away from the written route, you can make your way to the nearest point on the route card (using the technique of 'walking onto a boaring' if appropriate – see Chapter 15), at which point all the necessary navigation calculations are done for you. Navigation is easy when everything is going well – when you really need it there will be lots of other things going on in your mind, so the simpler you can make it, the better.

An example of one type of route card is shown in Figure 43. Note the wide variety of comments in the 'remarks' column, and how specific features have been located by grid references. Note also how each leg of the walk across trackless terrain is kept short in order to minimise the deviation resulting from any error.

Figure 43 | *Route card.*

This route card gives

details of a short

navigation exercise.

Front of card:

Date – 30/04/06		Start point – LAYBY ON B4560 @ 162160				
Feature	Grid Ref	M°	Dist	Ht ↑	Time	Remarks
QUARRY ENTRANCE	159162	–	600m	20m	11 mins	FOLLOW ROAD & TRACK
RING CONTOUR	155162	262	325m	30m	9 mins	UPHILL ALL THE WAY
POOL	152159	239	375m	–	7 mins	SHALLOW VALLEY N
TRIG POINT	147159	268	575 m	20u	13 mins	PATH 50m BEFORE
TWIN SHAKEHOLES	144156	220	400m	–	8 mins	FAIRLY FLAT
SHEEP SHELTER	139153	245	525m	–	11 mins	DOWNHILL ALL THE WAY
TWIN SHAKEHOLES	142148	160	500m	–	10 min	IN BASIN
SHAKEHOLE	148151	73	650m	<10m	13 mins	STREAM @ 400m
SHAKEHOLE	153151	85	500m	<10m	10 min	UNDULATING
POOL	157149	117	500m	–	10 mins	PATH 75m BEFORE
POOL	160151	63	375m	10m	8 mins	
POOL IN SHAKEHOLE	163153	62	375m	10m	8 mins	DRY SHAKEHOLE N
ROAD	–	45	150m	20m	5 mins	AIM OFF –TURN LEFT TO REGAIN START.

Back of card:

Size of party – 4 ADULTS
Estimate time of return – 1800 HRS
Escape Routes –
① HEAD DUE EAST TO ROAD

To recap

Route planning is simply deciding on where you are going for a day's walking, and can be done from the map. Route finding is the art of finding the easiest route between two points. It is a continuous process that is done on the ground, and requires practice.

Route cards are useful aids to safety and navigation, especially when conditions are poor. To be of any use, they should give all the necessary information in a clear and unambiguous way.

20 DIFFICULT SITUATIONS

A major part of the art of navigation lies in combining a number of different techniques to suit a particular set of circumstances. As a result, different people may well approach the same situation in totally different ways, which can be confusing to the beginner. However, this is how it should be, for personal preference plays an important role in successful navigation.

Confidence is also important. You need to be confident about not only your skills, but also your ability to get back to safety should the need arise. This is why regular practice is so important. Use every opportunity you can to practise all the basic techniques until they become comfortably familiar. Do not make the mistake of waiting until you need them for real!

Despite this advice, and no matter how experienced or well prepared you are, there are a number of situations in which both your skills and your confidence may well be put to the test. A few of the more common of these difficult situations are outlined below, together with suggested approaches.

Featureless terrain

It should be fairly obvious that a major problem when navigating through featureless terrain is that everything looks the same! It is not so much that there are no features – simply that all features look very much alike. Unless you are able to get some frame of reference (particularly in relation to height), it soon becomes difficult to judge whether a particular hummock is big enough to be reflected in the contour patterns. This is especially true when using BMC/Harvey maps in gently undulating moorland areas where, despite the auxiliary contours, the 15 metre contour interval can put you at a slight disadvantage. As was pointed out in Chapter 8, small bumps which break the contour line will be shown on your map, whereas large ones which don't break the contour line will not. Unless borne in mind, this can lead to unnecessary confusion!

Personally, I relish the experience of wandering across trackless moorland, and I don't really mind if I do not know exactly where I am all the time. I tend to make extensive use of a combination of handrails and aiming off, and often use linear features as **collecting features** that lead me towards where I wish to go. In the rare situations where this is not possible, I try to use high points (often shown as ring contours or spot heights) as physical waypoints, and navigate using these as features which allow me to 'walk onto a bearing' (as described in Chapter 15). In good visibility, I do this roughly rather than precisely by using a combination of setting the map and line of sight. This is a good illustration of how the art of navigation involves combining several techniques.

Photo 43 | *Featureless terrain can demand careful navigation, but should present few difficulties in visibility like this! Note the trig point in the distance.*

If things are particularly critical and the visibility is poor or unpredictable, it may be prudent to start from a known point and keep track of your position by using a combination of bearings and pacing.

Let's be honest – if you are standing in the middle of a gently undulating stretch of heather moorland in poor visibility, there is no way you can pinpoint your position unless: (a) you have been pacing along a bearing from a known point, or (b) you have a GPS device with you. However, if the landscape is featureless, does it really matter if you do not know exactly where you are? Can you not just head towards a convenient handrail and relocate from there? Whilst that is certainly one answer (others will be found in Chapter 25), what if something has happened and you need to pinpoint your position? Perhaps a companion has stumbled and snapped his ankle, and you need to get help. Again, it is the ability to combine various techniques that is important. In the absence of a GPS device, you will have to pinpoint your position by relating it to a known feature. You should know where you are to within a couple of kilometres or so, so you need to look at that rough area on your map and find some form of linear feature – the further away it is, the bigger it needs to be. Once you have decided on the feature, walk towards it following a definite compass bearing, and either pace or time the journey. Once you reach the handrail, follow it, again pacing or timing this new leg of your journey, until you reach a point where you can pinpoint your position. By referring back to the bearing and distance or time it took to reach this point, you should be able to relocate the accident site with a reasonable degree of accuracy (see Figure 44).

Figure 44 | Pinpointing location in featureless terrain.

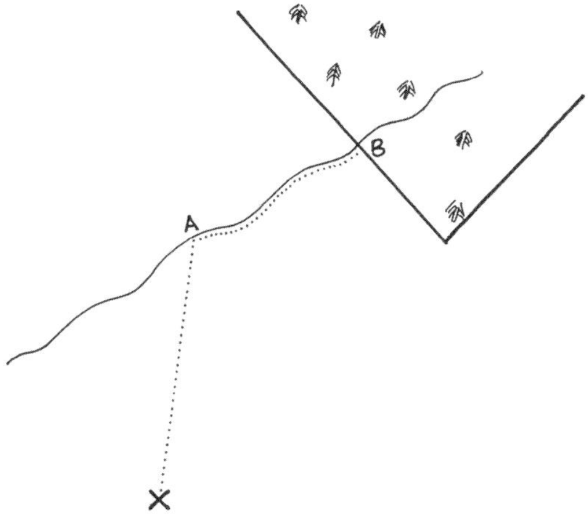

Night navigation

Navigating in the dark is little different to navigating in very poor visibility, and so similar considerations apply. However, be aware that your distance perception will be seriously affected because, even in clear visibility, the horizon may appear silhouetted in such a way that more distant features effectively camouflage those that are closer. Adhere to the KISS principle (see Chapter 22), make full use of handrails whenever possible, and think carefully about simplifying things by aiming off or using attack points before following a bearing. Good observation skills are essential – small things like changes in the nature of the terrain or alterations in the steepness or aspect of a slope can be extremely useful, and it will help if you get into the habit of setting the map correctly, every time you consult it.

A headtorch will prove invaluable, but try to keep its use to a minimum and navigate using night vision whenever possible. It takes a surprisingly long time for your eyes to adapt fully to the dark (just under an hour!), but they will revert to normal vision almost instantaneously if the light increases above a certain level. In order to preserve at least some of their night vision, many people close (or cover) one eye when looking at the map with a light. Although some people recommend putting a red filter on the torch (because red light does not affect night vision), in practice this is less than helpful when reading a map because it is virtually impossible to see contour lines in red light.

If you need to use your headtorch (as when, for example, crossing a boulder field), try to adjust the beam to minimise the danger of the glare affecting your eyes, and on those torches with adjustable light settings, use the minimum intensity conducive with safety. Try to avoid shining your head torch beam directly into your companions' eyes unless you want to become unpopular!

If you are forced to follow a precise bearing at night, you will find that it is extremely difficult, if not impossible, to find suitable spots on which to sight. Leapfrogging is therefore usually the preferred option, although you obviously cannot use this method if you are alone. If it is a very dark or misty night, the person on whom you sight may well have to show some kind of light – I carry a small pen-torch with a red filter for just this eventuality, and some head torches have a red light option that is useful in this situation. If it is a clear night, it is often possible to use a star as a sighting spot. Choose one low on the horizon and make sure you can recognise it again – on a crisp, cold, clear night, the number of stars in the sky above the mountains (where there is little if any light pollution) can be breathtaking. On longer legs of navigation, bear in mind that stars are not stationary with respect to the horizon (apart from the Pole Star which appears not to move), so you should change your point of reference at least once every 10 to 15 minutes.

Winter conditions

Navigating during the winter months is little different from any other time of year, with two important exceptions. Firstly, because winter days are shorter and the weather conditions potentially more severe, accurate navigation is even more critical than at other times. Secondly, if the landscape is covered by a blanket of snow, you will need to consider a whole host of additional factors. Whilst a discussion of winter mountain safety is way beyond the scope of this book, a few pointers are highly relevant.

A layer of snow can soften and smooth the shape of the landscape, potentially hiding several of the features that you might use during warmer months. This means that some of the detail shown on OS Explorer maps may not be visible, and for this reason many people prefer to use either BMC/Harvey maps (on which the 15 metre contour interval 'smoothes' the landscape to a certain degree), or OS Landranger maps, where a certain amount of contour information has already been simplified. Whichever type or scale you decide to use, make sure your map is weatherproof, either by using a laminated map, or by folding your map into a good quality map case.

Photo 44 | *Snow can smooth and soften the landscape.*

When route planning and route finding, make as much use as possible of handrails, attack points and physical waypoints, and bear in mind that snow can effectively camouflage both helpful and unhelpful features. For example, crossing boggy areas with a light covering of snow over ice can be a nightmare – the snow can hide the pools and you can easily end up breaking through the ice and getting a boot full of freezing water, or worse! Boulder fields, too, can be exhausting, the snow hiding boot-swallowing, ankle-wrenching gaps between the boulders. You should also be careful when choosing destinations – small streams and pools can freeze over and then become invisible beneath a layer of snow, top edges of cliffs (and even relatively small outcrops) can be masked by potentially lethal cornices, and convex slopes can be avalanche prone. You need to be very aware of your surroundings, not so much in terms of pinpoint features (many of which may be hidden), but more in terms of shape. Be observant in terms of changes in the gradient or aspect of slopes, and look out for local contour features such as ring contours, small valleys and spurs, breaks of slope, slight reascents, etc.

Using spotting to follow precise bearings when there is deep snow on the ground can be virtually impossible, so leapfrogging or "walking on the needle" may be better options. However, if you are unlucky enough to be caught in true whiteout conditions, even leapfrogging can become problematic, so you will need to use handrails whenever possible. Many people believe they have experienced whiteout when, in fact, they have simply been in very thick mist! True whiteout is rare south of the Scottish border, and can only occur when there is snow both in the air and on the ground. The phenomenon occurs because there is no horizon whatsoever – you cannot see whether the ground in front of you rises, falls or stays level, and your companions will appear to float. In these conditions, many people spend a considerable amount of time stumbling or falling over! Blizzard conditions can be even more trying. It is impossible to retreat into the face of a true blizzard – you either have to find shelter (an extremely serious undertaking for the ill-equipped), or retreat with your back to the wind before it gets too bad.

Photo 45 | *Winter conditions can make navigation extremely difficult.*

Because conditions can be so severe, it is vital to use the KISS principle (see Chapter 22). Keep each leg of navigation as short as possible, double-check (or even treble-check) all your bearings (and get a companion to do the same), use a romer scale to measure distances from the map, and use speed/time and distance/pace grids to help you with your time and distance estimates.

Ridge-line scrambling

Aside from whiteout and blizzard conditions, one of the trickiest scenarios is navigating along a rocky ridge in thick mist. In this situation, both timing and pacing can be problematic, and the use of the compass can be limited by the nature of the terrain. Good map interpretation is, as ever, the real key to success. Before setting out, make a point of studying the map carefully in order to identify the main features of the ridge. Look in particular for changes of direction and in the angle or aspect of the slopes, major buttresses and gullies, spot heights, and subsidiary ridges. When moving, be aware of your surroundings, and be observant with respect to your direction of travel and the angle and aspect of slopes.

Photo 46 | *It can be difficult to get a precise location when scrambling on rocky ridges. If the ridge twists and turns, aspect of slope may help.*

Even the most detailed 1:25,000 scale map cannot show all the intricacies of a complex ridge. Indeed, sometimes the amount of detail that is shown simply has the effect of making the map confusing. This is especially true of OS maps (and particularly Explorer maps), where symbols for such things as outcrop, boulders and vertical faces can effectively mask the contours, thus making it extremely difficult to interpret the precise shape of the land. BMC and Harvey Superwalker maps are usually easier to interpret in this situation, not only because prominent boulders and outcrops are clearly shown in their precise positions, but also because the larger vertical interval simplifies the intricacies of the landscape, and bouldery or rocky areas are shown simply by changing the colour of the contours from brown to grey, rather than plastering the map with more symbols. Be aware, too, that smaller scale maps can be useful if you wish to get a general idea of the shape.

Several other things may help. If, for example, the ridge twists and turns, you can use your compass to measure the direction of the ridge at any particular point, and then transfer this information to the map. Point the DOT arrow along the ridge, take a magnetic bearing in the normal way, convert it to a grid bearing, and then place the compass on the map so that the orienting arrow points to the top of the map and the orienting lines run parallel to the north-south grid lines. Now compare the direction shown by the DOT arrow with orientation of the ridge, and look for places where the directions coincide (see also Chapter 15).

Knowing your height above sea level can be extremely helpful, but this can be very difficult to judge without reference to something else. If the visibility is good enough, you might be able to compare your height with a definite feature of known height on a neighbouring peak, but judging height in this way is not as foolproof as it may appear, and significantly large errors are common (see Chapter 23). It is in this type of situation that an **altimeter** can be extremely useful. Wristwatch altimeters are now widely available, and many are extremely accurate as long as you understand their limitations, as outlined below. Indeed, a correctly calibrated wrist-watch altimeter will give you a far more reliable and accurate height than many GPS devices.

Photo 47 | *An altimeter will help you get a precise location in situations like this.*

Altimeters use changes in atmospheric pressure to calculate height, based upon the fact that the higher you climb, the lower the atmospheric pressure. However, changes in atmospheric pressure are also caused by the weather, and significant inaccuracies can occur unless these weather factors are taken into consideration. The easiest way around this is to calibrate your altimeter at the start of the day, just before you start walking, then to check it regularly by comparing the height shown with the actual height at known points along the route – trig points and spot heights being the two most common examples. This also has the benefit of alerting you to possible weather changes, for if the altimeter continually shows a height which is significantly greater than the actual height (especially if you have been correcting it at regular intervals), it means that the atmospheric pressure is dropping and that the weather is likely to deteriorate.

As with your compass, the uses of an altimeter are limited solely by your imagination. In addition to giving you extra information that might be of help when trying to pinpoint your position, it can also be used to gauge your progress, and can be extremely useful when, for example, you need to leave a ridge at a particular height which is not readily apparent from features on the ground (see Figure 45).

An altimeter should be regarded as an essential item of equipment if you intend to walk abroad in areas where there are glaciers. Because the ice is constantly flowing, it is impossible to map a glacier accurately, so being able to work out your height at any given point is extremely helpful.

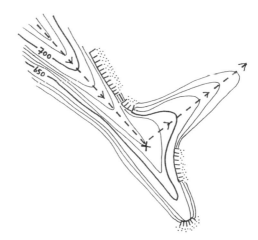

Figure 45 | *Using an altimeter to help calculate a cut-off point.*

Traversing – following contours

A contour can be thought of as an invisible linear feature, which means it can be used as a handrail. This is easiest to do when there is an obvious horizontal break of slope, where the angle of the slope changes significantly (see Photo 16). Unfortunately, however, not all breaks of slope are horizontal, and contour lines are usually invisible.

Most people find it extremely difficult to remain at a precise height when traversing or moving across an otherwise blank slope, especially in poor visibility. Some people gain height whilst others lose it – there seems to be no hard-and-fast rule. An altimeter will obviously be helpful in this situation, but there are other things that will help you follow a level course. The simplest of these is to sight on an object that lies towards the limit of visibility, and then walk towards it – just like following a bearing by spotting. If you have a walking pole, sighting along it will help – especially if you get a companion to ensure that it is horizontal. If the visibility is particularly poor, make sure that the object remains at eye level when you reach it – if you stand on it, you will be gaining height. Although you may feel that this error will be negligible, if the visibility is 25 metres and you traverse a distance of 500 metres, you could climb more than 30 metres unless you consider this 'eye level' error.

Even where you manage to maintain a level path, it can be very difficult to keep track of your progress when following contours. Accurate pacing and/or careful time estimations will certainly help, but unless the slope is perfectly smooth, the error factors can be significant. Wherever possible, try to head towards some form of handrail such as a stream that will limit your progress and act as a collecting feature. Once reached, you then follow it (as if you had been aiming off) in order to reach a known or identifiable point.

Finally, when faced with a steep climb over a short spur, consider the possibility that it may be quicker and easier to walk around it. Use Naismith's Rule to calculate times for both the direct route and the roundabout, but more level, route, and see which is quicker. You will often be surprised! (see Figure 46).

Figure 46 | *Over or around?*

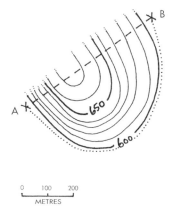

163

To recap

There are a number of scenarios in which both your navigational skill and your confidence may be put to the test, the main ones being: crossing featureless terrain, navigating at night, navigating in winter conditions when there is snow on the ground, and ridgeline scrambling in poor visibility. Successful navigation in these situations requires good map interpretation combined with familiarity with all the various techniques, which then allows you to make considered judgments about when to use what combination of techniques to suit which particular set of circumstances.

Although contour lines can be used in the same way as linear features, the fact that they are invisible poses a number of potential problems, not the least of which is that most people find it extremely difficult to maintain a constant height when traversing.

21 PRACTICE MAKES PERFECT

You will, by now, have realised that I am constantly encouraging you to get as much practice as possible of all the individual navigation techniques, before you need to use them for real. Simply knowing how to do it is not enough – you need to be so familiar and comfortable with each individual skill that you hardly have to think about what you are doing. I am not for one moment suggesting that you should use pinpoint map interpretation and follow timed or paced bearings every time you go out, but I would encourage you to practise at least one technique for every leg of navigation, each time you go for a walk, even in perfect conditions. In this way you will be far more confident about using the techniques in situations where getting it wrong could be disastrous.

There is no such thing as an 'expert' navigator. Even now, after all the years that I have been teaching navigation, I am not an 'expert' – I am simply very experienced! Each time I go for a walk, whether for my own enjoyment or that of others, I make sure I practise at least one aspect of navigation at some point. This may involve doing some map interpretation when I stop for lunch, working out a time for a journey between two known points and then seeing how accurate it was, measuring a distance between two points and then pacing it, or following a bearing to a hidden spot. There are so many opportunities to practise without needing to make it a chore.

Practising map interpretation

Even if you live in a heavily built-up area, there are plenty of things that you can do to practise your map interpretation. For example, if you don't already have one, buy yourself a 1:25,000 scale map that has your house on it, then do the exercise I asked you to do earlier using Map 6, not just for the grid square that contains your house, but also for all the adjacent squares. If your map interpretation is good enough, I can virtually guarantee that you will find out something about your home area that you didn't know! Of course, you do know your home area to a large extent, so doing this exercise will help you gain a better appreciation of how maps portray shape, size and distance.

Photo 48 | *If you stop for lunch with views like this, use the opportunity to practise your map interpretation.*

Practising bearings and pacing

Obviously, it is easier to practise compass work if you live in the country than if you live in a town or city, but there are still things you can do, especially if you can find an open area such as a sports field or a park. Perhaps the most useful is to walk regular geometric patterns using a combination of compass work and pacing. This is also a great way to introduce children to compass navigation.

What you need is a large open area (the larger, the better), preferably with longish grass. Parks and playing fields are ideal. Put something on the ground in such a way that you can only see it when you are virtually standing over it – sweets are ideal as they give you some incentive, but avoid using coins or anything valuable as you may well lose them! What you are going to

START

Walk 360° for 100 metres

Walk 120° for 100 metres

Walk 240° for 100 metres

Figure 47 | *Walking a regular geometric shape.*

Area from within which the objective is visible.

START

>>> Back bearing >>>

>>> Forward bearing >>>

Figure 48 | *Checking for consistent errors.*

do is use a combination of bearings and pacing to walk a regular geometric shape, the easiest being an equilateral triangle because you only have to get three 'legs' correct. In this example, starting from the object you are using as the incentive, walk on a bearing of 120° for 100 metres, then turn and follow a bearing of 240° for 100 metres, then turn again and follow a bearing of 360° for 100 metres. If you have been accurate, you will be standing precisely at your start point and can retrieve your incentive! This is shown graphically in Figure 47.

The maths are easy – you simply divide 360° by the number of legs you wish to follow, then make each leg exactly the same length. You can divide 360° by four to give you bearings of 90°, 180°, 270° and 360°, which would result in you walking a perfect square; you can divide 360° by five and walk a pentagon, by six and walk a hexagon, and so on. The more legs there are, the harder it is to be precise, but as long as you keep each leg the same length, you should always end up at your start point. Once you get more complex than a square, don't use 100 metres as the distance unless you have a huge area to work with – start using 50 metres per leg or maybe even less.

If you find this exercise difficult and regularly end up losing your incentive, it means that either your compass technique or your pacing technique needs refining. To discover which it is, find yourself as large an area as possible, and put something on the ground that you can still see from a reasonable distance. Now, starting from that point, walk on any bearing you like for as far as you reasonably can, pacing the distance; then turn around 180° and follow the back bearing for precisely the same distance. If you end up to one side of your origin point, it is your compass technique that needs attention; if you end up short of your original point (or past it), it is your pacing technique that needs attention. This is shown graphically in Figure 48.

You may find that you get this exercise right whilst getting the earlier geometric shape exercise wrong, in which case it means that you are making a consistent error. This can happen, for example, when people suffer from astigmatism (an eye condition) or have a particularly dominant foot, as mentioned in Chapter 15. If this is the case, the only way to find out whether the error is with the bearing or the pacing is to get a companion to stand a short distance away and to follow exactly the same bearing for precisely the same distance. If you veer away from one another, the error is with the bearing; if you stay parallel but end up walking different distances, the error is with the pacing.

Once you have identified the error, it is then easier to correct it.

To recap

It is really important to practise all the navigation techniques on a regular basis, and before you need them for real. This can be done in many ways, even if you live in a heavily built-up area.

PART 4 – SO YOU THINK YOU'RE LOST?

In this final part of the book, I am going to show you how to minimise the chances of becoming 'locationally challenged' by using the KISS principle, to explain how your eyes can give you false information about your surroundings, and to describe some simple methods of searching for that illusive objective. We are also going to look at the art of **relocation** – arguably the most important aspect of wilderness navigation.

No matter how careful or diligent you are, if you walk regularly there will almost certainly come a time when, with a horrible sinking feeling, you slowly come to the realisation that you haven't the faintest idea where you are! It is in situations such as this that the art of relocation comes into its own, allowing you to work out where you are by using the best combination of techniques to suit the particular set of circumstances in which you find yourself.

22 KISS

Keeping it short and simple

Poor visibility navigation is an exercise in damage limitation – the further you go, the greater the potential error. It therefore makes perfect sense for you to keep each leg of navigation as *short* as possible. However, there are other factors to consider, because when accurate navigation is critical, your head is likely be full of lots of other thoughts. It therefore makes perfect sense for you to keep things as *simple* as possible as well – if only for your peace of mind. This is known as the KISS principle – Keep It Short and Simple – and I consider it one of the most important factors in successful and pain-free navigation!

Let me try to give you some perspective. Imagine that you are on gently undulating moorland in thick mist, following a bearing from point A to point B – a distance of one kilometre. A 1° error over this distance will put you about 20 metres off course. A 3° error will therefore put you about 60 metres off course. Whilst this error factor may not seem large, if you have visibility of 50 metres or less, you have a problem, for you have little chance of seeing your objective. Moreover, you will probably have no idea to which side of you your objective lies – it could be 60 metres to the left or to the right – so that small 3° error effectively results in a 'grey area' of 120 metres. If you combine this with a potential 5% error in your distance estimation (equal to +/- 50 metres over that same kilometre distance), your target could be anywhere within a 'grey area' of 12,000 square metres – an area equal to twice the size of a football pitch!

In order to minimise your errors, whenever you are in poor visibility and away from good paths, and particularly when you are crossing featureless moorland or open mountainside, keep each leg of navigation as short as possible. If your map interpretation is good, legs of 500 metres or less should be possible in most areas. What we are talking about here is micro-navigation – making as much use as possible of the incredible detail shown on the map. For quick reference, when you are calculating a bearing using a 1:25,000 scale map, if the lines in your compass base plate are getting too short to reach easily between the two points on the map, you are going too far. Where you are forced to go further due to the featureless nature of the terrain, always try to head towards some form of linear feature which lies across your path, and which you can eventually use as a handrail to take you to a definite point.

Keeping each leg of navigation short is just one aspect of the KISS principle – keeping the navigation simple is equally important. Get into the habit of using either a sheet magnifier or the lens on your compass when interpreting your map, and try to find the *easiest* way to reach your target – this will not necessarily be the *shortest* or the *quickest* route. Navigate using handrails and collecting features whenever possible (see Chapter 20), and make use of romer scales, speed/time and distance/pace grids to minimise the amount of mental arithmetic you have to do.

You can also limit the possibility of error by using a **catching feature**. This is simply any prominent feature that lies a short distance beyond your intended goal. This can be useful, even though you do not plan to walk to it, simply because if you arrive at it, you know you have overshot your objective. It is then a simple matter to return the short distance to your destination. Using catching features reduces the possibility of wandering aimlessly in the hope that you are still on track. Knowing there is a catching feature ahead also means you can proceed more confidently towards your destination, knowing that if you go too far you will be 'caught'.

Photo 49 | *KISS – Keep It Short and Simple!*

When using bearings in poor visibility, think carefully about the type of feature you choose as an objective, and about how you are going to calculate your bearing. If, for example, you are heading to a pool, make sure your bearing runs right through the middle of it. In this way, even if you make a small error, you still have a good chance of seeing it. Conversely, when heading away from a pool, or from any feature which covers an area, it is important that you choose a precise point from where you are going to leave this feature and take your bearing from there. If, for example, you take a bearing from the north side of a pool which is 100 metres across, but then leave the pool from the south side, you are following a **parallel bearing** and are already 100 metres off course (see Figure 49).

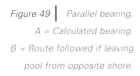 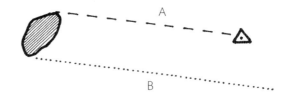

Figure 49 | *Parallel bearing.*
A = Calculated bearing.
B = Route followed if leaving
pool from opposite shore.

It also makes perfect sense to double- or even treble-check everything. This applies as much to your choice of route and your estimations of time and distance as it does to your bearings. Whenever possible, get at least two people to do the same calculations and then check that the results agree. When calculating bearings, most people can estimate angles to within 20° or so, and you can easily check that you have not made a common 90° error by 'checking the quadrants' (see Chapter 11 and Figure 18).

If you apply the KISS principle every time you find yourself in poor visibility or featureless terrain, you will minimise your chances of straying too far off course. However, everyone makes mistakes, so the rest of this part of the book is concerned with those occasions when, for some inexplicable reason, you find yourself 'locationally challenged'!

To recap

Particularly in poor visibility, it is important to adhere to the KISS principle – Keep It Short and Simple. This means keeping each leg of navigation as short as possible between known points, and keeping the route and calculations as simple as possible.

You should also get into the habit of double-checking everything.

23 YOUR EYES CAN LIE

Poor visibility can make your eyes do funny things! For example, it can become extremely difficult to judge distance and depth, and it is all too easy to imagine that you can see things that are not there. This is one of the reasons that, whenever you try to work out your position, it is always better to start by working from the ground to the map. If you work the other way around, trying to relate the mass of information you can obtain from the map to the small amount of information that you can see on the ground, you run the risk that you will 'make things fit'.

We will look at the sequence of events that make up relocation in more detail in Chapter 25. However, even when looking at landscape in perfect visibility, there are a number of situations in which your eyes can mislead you, and an awareness of these will obviously be helpful.

The further you look – the flatter the landscape appears

One of the more common mistakes made by people when they are trying to work out their position in reasonable visibility is that they look too far away. The problem is that the further away you look, the flatter the landscape becomes, and it is surprisingly easy to lose all sense of depth and perspective. Distance can cause curving headwalls to appear flat; can make two summits that actually lie one behind the other to appear as if they are side by side; and can

make a sinuously curving cliff look like a straight escarpment. Particularly when it is dull, but also on cloudless days when the sun is high, landscape features can merge in such a way that distant ridges separated by two or three kilometres can appear to be one continuous feature. When relocating, therefore, unless you are absolutely certain that you can positively identify a distant feature, always start by looking at the near landscape rather than the far horizons.

We don't judge distance – we judge size

Many of even the most experienced people find that judging distance can often be tricky, even in good visibility. The problem is that, as humans, we all have relatively poor stereoscopic vision, simply because our eyes are so close together! In order to compensate for this, the method our brain uses to judge distance is to look at relative size. In practice, what this means is that if, for example, we look across a stretch of moorland and see a car, we can usually get a reasonable impression of its distance from us, simply because we know the size of a car. However, if we look across the same stretch of moorland and see a boulder, it is far more difficult to judge its distance, simply because we do not know the size of the boulder.

This can also work the other way, because your brain will sometimes make assumptions about the distance and alter the perceived size of an object accordingly. A good example of this often occurs on the moors near my home, when people mistake white ponies for sheep (and vice versa)!

The further away the horizon, the smaller the local landscape appears

Another way your eyes can lie is related to the distance to the horizon. In basic terms, the further away the horizon, the smaller the appearance of the local landscape, whereas the closer the horizon, the larger the appearance of the local landscape. In effect, if you have fantastic visibility of 50 kilometres, the local lumps and bumps of the landscape will seem insignificant, whereas if you have poor visibility of 50 metres, the same lumps and bumps will appear to be much bigger. This has the effect of making it difficult to judge size, shape and distance in poor visibility, and particularly in those situations where the mist comes and goes. It also means that if you are following a linear route and the visibility deteriorates during the day, the landscape you perceive in poor visibility during the return journey will look different to the landscape seen in good visibility during your outward journey – even though you are retracing your steps across known ground.

Photo 51 | *How far down? Not as far as most people think! It is often difficult to judge depth.*

The rule of thirds

The most difficult situation in which to judge distance is when you are on (or are approaching) sloping ground, because this is precisely the environment in which your eyes will tell the biggest lies. In basic terms, when you look up a slope, you perceive the landscape as being foreshortened, whereas when you look down a slope, you perceive it as being elongated. This effect is actually far more marked than many people realise. As a guide, when trying to judge distance in sloping terrain, remember the **rule of thirds**, as follows:

When looking up a slope – what you perceive to be halfway *up* the slope is actually only about one third of the way up – which explains why, at the start of the day, you look up the initial slopes and think you'll be up there in no time, whereas in reality, you're still toiling away an hour later!

When looking down a slope – what you perceive to be halfway *down* the slope is actually about two-thirds of the way down – which explains why, at the end of the day, you look down the slope and see your car, still miles away in the car park, whereas in reality, you seem to get back to it remarkably quickly.

These effects can occur on any type of slope – regular, concave or convex – despite the fact that it is difficult to see very far up or down a convex slope.

Whilst there appears to be no scientific basis for the rule of thirds, which means it should not be regarded as a precise measurement, it does act as a very useful rule of thumb.

Photo 52 | *Faces in the mist. Mist can do funny things to your eyes and can alter views in unexpected ways! These faces are not at all obvious in clear visibility.*

Poor light magnifies misperceptions

Finally, all these misperceptions are exacerbated by poor light, which means that they tend to be magnified in poor visibility and also at dusk. Indeed, as the light starts to decline, so our ability to judge depth becomes significantly reduced. I would hazard a guess that the stumbles taken when following a steep descent route at dusk are often caused as much (if not more) by failing depth perception as by tiredness at the end of a long day!

To recap

There are a number of situations in which your eyes can lie to you, particularly when trying to judge distance. This is most marked when looking up or down slopes, and is exacerbated by both poor visibility and poor light.

The rule of thirds, whilst not precise, is useful as a guide when looking up or down a slope.

24 SEARCHES

Unless you are very lucky, if you walk with any regularity there will almost inevitably come a time when you find yourself at the end of a paced or timed bearing in thick mist with no sign of your destination. It may well be that what you seek is only just out of sight in the mist, in which case a quick search will reveal it. However, wandering around randomly in the hope that you might stumble across your objective is far from the best approach, and will probably do little more than make matters worse. As with all other aspects of navigation, there is a definite art to searching.

The first thing to realise is that the bearing you have been following is important, even if it is wrong, simply because you may be able to follow it back to where you started by using a back bearing. No matter what search method you use, it should therefore be done in such a way that you can always get back onto the line of your bearing.

With this in mind, not only are the following three search methods all comparatively simple, but they also allow you to regain your original bearing at the point at which you made the decision to search.

Line search

The simplest form of search is the **line search** (see Figure 50). In this method, one person stays on the line of the bearing (and continues pacing if appropriate), whilst the remainder of the party spread out to either side. The distance between each person will depend upon not only the visibility, but also the nature of both the terrain and the objective. Do not forget that visibility can deteriorate suddenly, so do not simply place people at the limit of visibility – make sure they move back into sight by at least a few metres. With the exception of the people at either end of the line (who will only be able to see one other person), everyone should have a clear view of both their neighbours, and of the terrain separating them.

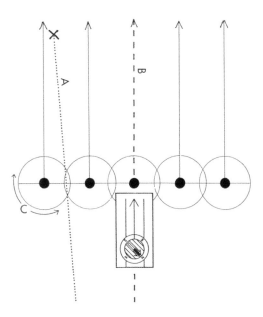

Figure 50 | Line Search.
A = Intended course.
B = Actual course.
C = Limit of visibility.

For reasons that should be obvious, this type of search is more efficient, the more people there are in the party. It is also more effective if started well before reaching the end of the bearing in order to reduce the possibility that the objective has already been passed before the search is initiated. If this latter scenario is thought likely, the line search can be used in conjunction with a back bearing whilst retracing the outward route.

Rotational sweep search

Rotational sweep searches (see Figure 51) can be an effective way of recovering from slight errors of navigation. As with line searches, the greater the number of people in the party, the more efficient the search. However, unlike the line search, which should either be started early, or in conjunction with a back bearing whilst retracing your steps, rotational sweep searches are more effective when done once the destination should have been reached, but nothing can be seen of it. They are particularly useful if used in conjunction with time windows (as described in Chapter 13), the search pattern being centred on the position reached at the optimum time.

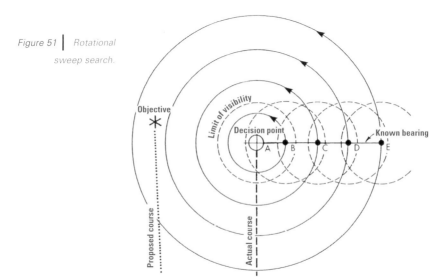

Figure 51 | Rotational sweep search.

The basic idea is for the party to spread out in a line. As with line searches, each person (except the two people at either end of the line) should be able to see both their neighbours, and the distance between each person will depend not only upon the visibility, but also upon the nature of both the terrain and the objective. Unlike line searches, however, the line of people is formed to one side of the bearing only, with the person at the near end of the line standing at the exact spot reached when the decision to search was taken (or at the position reached at the optimum time). The pivot point or axis of rotation is thus centred on the bearing that was being followed so that, as a last resort, you can always retrace your steps using a back bearing.

The person standing at the pivot point should now take a compass bearing along the line of people (this will be important later if the objective is not found), after which the whole line moves, pivoting around the central point until, if you're lucky, the objective is found. Don't forget that those people furthest away from the centre will have to travel a considerably greater distance than those people nearer the centre, so it is important that this type of search is carefully controlled and is undertaken in a disciplined way. If, after a full sweep of 360° (at which point the line of people will be back on the bearing taken by the pivot person) the target still has not been sighted, you will have to think back very carefully to see if you can identify any potential error in your navigation. If you still believe that you are close to your objective, you can carry out an **expanding spiral search**, as described below.

Expanding spiral search

Expanding spiral searches are useful not only in those situations where the previous search patterns have failed, but also when there are only a few people in the party. Indeed, this method of searching can be conducted solo, yet still allows the decision point to be regained should the objective not be found after a predetermined time or distance. Although it may appear complicated at first glance, it is actually quite straightforward – once you get your head around the geometry!

The search pattern is based on a grid system (as illustrated in Figure 52), and uses forward bearings, back bearings, box bearings and pacing to follow a structured course. In order to keep things simple (and thus adhere to the KISS principle), it is helpful to have some means of recording your progress, such as a laminated map and a Chinagraph pencil, or a waterproof notebook and pencil.

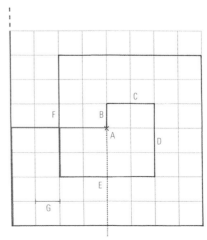

Figure 52 | *Expanding spiral search.*
A = Decision point.
B = Forward bearing.
C = Box bearing.
D = Back bearing.
E = Reverse box bearing.
F = Original bearing.
G = Set distance.
Red line = route taken to regain the decision point.

To start the search, leave the decision point along the bearing you were following, continuing for a distance equal to just short of the limit of visibility. The easiest way to decide on this distance is to send a companion on in front until they just reach the limit of visibility. You then walk towards them, counting paces, and stopping just before you reach them at a convenient (easy to remember) number of paces. This becomes your **set distance**. It is important that you remember the number of paces! Now turn clockwise by 90° and follow a box bearing for a distance equivalent to twice the set distance (e.g. count the required number of paces twice). Now turn clockwise again by a further 90° onto a back bearing, and follow this for a distance equivalent to three times the set distance; then clockwise again onto another box bearing for a distance of four times the set distance, and so on. Each time you have travelled the required number of set distances, you turn clockwise by 90° and add a further set distance to the next leg of the search. This sequence should be obvious from Figure 52.

Although you have to leave your original bearing when using this search pattern, the fact that you are using a constant set distance and turning by 90° each time means that it is relatively straightforward to regain the decision point if you do not find your objective within an acceptable time. This is easier to do if you draw the search pattern in a grid format, similar to that in the illustration. It is also possible to regain the decision point after every fourth expansion (i.e. each second box bearing) by turning clockwise by 90°, pacing half the distance of your last leg, then turning clockwise by 90° again and pacing the same distance.

Other considerations

When using any search technique, it is important that you consider the nature of the terrain, particularly with regard to any potential hazards. For example, if you are walking in the mountains in winter conditions with snow and ice on the ground, you need to ask whether there may be cornices in the area. If so, it may be advisable to rope up. Similarly, if you are searching for any type of water feature, it may be thinly frozen and then hidden under a thin covering of snow – potentially a lethal combination.

No matter what the season, because the party will be spread out in such a way that not all members will be able to see all other members, communication will become extremely difficult, so it is a good idea to appoint one person to co-ordinate the search. The very fact that you have found it necessary to search will almost certainly have affected morale, and some people may be very apprehensive. Confusion is easy, and mistakes are potentially quite

Photo 53 | *In winter conditions, pools can sometimes be hidden under snow-covered ice – potentially a lethal combination.*

costly. I wonder how many times someone has shouted, "Here it is!", whereupon everyone has come running, only to find that it is not the correct position after all! But now you have lost your decision point and thus cannot regain your bearing!

To recap

If you get to the end of your bearing and have not found your objective, a simple search will often reveal it. All searches should be done in a methodical way, with due regard to the nature of the terrain and any potential hazards. The more people there are in a party, the more effective will be the search.

No matter what search method you use, you should always be able to get back to your original bearing so that, if necessary, you can use a back bearing to retrace your steps to the start of that leg of navigation.

25 THE ART OF RELOCATION

Good navigators are never lost! They may be 'temporarily mislocated', or even 'locationally challenged', but they are *never* lost!

Even if you are unsure about the accuracy of this statement, I believe it is of vital importance that you appreciate just how much your mental attitude will affect your decisions when, for some reason that is totally inexplicable at the time, you realise that you have absolutely no idea where you are. You may be an experienced and hitherto successful navigator, but if you walk with any regularity it is an odds-on certainty that you will eventually make a mistake. Unless you are prepared for the eventuality, it will come as rather a shock.

Relocation is not a science, it is an art – one which relies on a general familiarity with all the skills mentioned in this book, combined with keen observation. Moreover, it is not a haphazard affair – no matter what the circumstances, there is a definite sequence of events that should be followed in order to aid success. Without doubt, the first thing you should do when you think you might be lost is to tell yourself that you are *not* lost; no matter what you have been doing or where you are walking, you will almost certainly know where you are to within a few kilometres. If you know how to estimate time, you can probably be even more accurate.

The initial and almost irresistible temptation will be to stare at your map, hoping for inspiration. Unfortunately, this is totally the wrong thing to do because you cannot work out your position simply by staring at a map. What you must do, no matter how poor the visibility, is obtain information from the ground. So, having told yourself that you are *not* lost, and having resisted the temptation to stare at the map, slowly and deliberately turn around through 360° in order to get as much information as possible from the ground that is visible. Don't just glance over your shoulder; turn around completely – it is frighteningly easy to miss things if you just glance over your shoulder. Indeed, I have known people miss seeing a trig point that was less than 20 metres away simply because it was directly behind them!

Once you believe you have got as much information as possible from the ground (this may involve turning round several times), face the direction that you believe to be the most significant, and then set your map with your compass so that everything on the map is in the same orientation as everything on the ground. The reason you face the most significant direction before setting the map is that if you set it facing in another direction, there is a danger that the map will move with you when you turn to look at the significant features, thus becoming 'unset'. In any event, it is prudent to hold your compass on the map so that you can regularly check its alignment with north.

Photo 54 | *Keeping map and compass together to aid setting the map.*

Once your map is set, you can then start relating the things you can see on the ground to the features shown on the map. If you start by relating ground to map rather than map to ground, you are far less likely to 'make things fit'!

It will also be helpful to think back over your journey, trying to recall any features you may have passed, the nature of the terrain, and the aspect and steepness of any slopes that you have recently crossed. In essence, what you are aiming to do is to build up a mental picture of the wider surroundings, layer by layer (see Chapter 8), and then transfer this mental picture to the map. Once you have done this, you will be in a far better position to work out where you are.

Two additional points are worth noting. First, unless you have a GPS device, there is absolutely no way you can pinpoint your position in poor visibility when standing on a featureless mountainside or in the middle of a blank piece of moorland. In order to work out a precise location, you must be standing by a definite feature which is visible both on the map and on the ground.

Second, relocation is all about negatives! It is often far easier to work out **where you are not** than where you are, and this means that working out your position commonly involves a process of elimination. In navigation terms, knowing that you are definitely *not* somewhere is very positive! If, for example, there are only five places that you can possibly be and you can work out that you are definitely not at four of them, you know where you are! Some people seem to have difficulty in getting their heads around this idea of working with negatives.

Photo 55 | *When relocating in the mist, the shape of the land often gives you important information.*

Particularly in poor visibility, the best way to avoid becoming 'locationally challenged' is to keep your map handy and relate it to the ground at regular intervals. Be observant – keep looking around and make the most of any sudden increases in visibility, breaks in the cloud, or windows in the mist to get as much information about your surroundings as possible. Be aware of such things as changes in the aspect or steepness of slopes, and of anything else that will help you stay up-to-date with your position on the map, and try to maintain a constantly developing mental picture of the ground you are crossing.

So much for the basic theory and sequence of events. Let us now consider a couple of examples in order to see how this works in practice.

Example 1

In the first example, you are following a faint but obvious path across a relatively featureless stretch of hillside. The visibility, whilst not good, is reasonable, and noticing in the distance what appears to be a potentially interesting viewpoint, you leave the path and head straight towards it, your back to the wind. Unnoticed behind you, the cloud base is dropping rapidly, and before you realise what is happening you find yourself overtaken by thick mist. According to all the textbooks (including this one), you should have been observant enough to realise what was happening before the cloud arrived, but you weren't – it happens!

First things first – the worst thing you can do is panic. Rushing around in search of something recognisable will only make matters worse! It is far better take things slowly and approach the problem logically, so stop where you are and try to make life easy by asking a series of pertinent questions. For example:

If you turn around and walk into the wind, is the path you recently left well enough defined for you to recognise it easily when you reach it? If so, are you certain that the path runs at a sharp enough angle to your direction of approach and for a long enough distance that there is no danger that you might miss it? And if you do regain the path, how does that help you?

Alternatively, if you continue on your present heading, is your objective (the potentially inter-esting viewpoint) well enough defined that you will instantly recognise it when you reach it? If so, is it large enough that there is no danger that you might miss it altogether? And if you do find it, how does that help you?

If you can answer "yes" to either of the two questions above and you are certain of the direc-tion, you can travel back to the path or onwards to the objective. However, for the purposes of example, let us work on the basis that either you cannot answer "yes", or (more likely) you *think* you can, and then spend the next half hour or so trying unsuccessfully to find the path or the objective. What now?

Tell yourself that you are not lost – simply 'locationally challenged'. As mentioned above, if you stay calm and think logically, you should be able to work out where you are to within a couple of kilometres – so 95% or more of the map is immediately irrelevant. That is the same as saying that you only need concern yourself with 5% or less of the map, so concentrate just on that area.

The cloud is now claustrophobic, and you can only see about twenty metres. Once again, don't panic! Approach things logically and systematically.

Use *all* your senses:

Look! What is the ground like? All Explorer maps give you an indication of the nature of the terrain, so if you are in the middle of a boulder field, you cannot be in a grassy area on the map; if you are surrounded by heather, you cannot be in an area of rough grassland, and so on.

Listen! You can sometimes get clues from noise. Can you hear running water? Or the wind in trees? Or other people? Granted other people may be just as 'locationally challenged' as you, but they may have additional information that will be of help!

Sniff the air! Particularly in heavy mist, you can often smell pine woods, bracken, bogs, etc.

Feel the wind! Are you facing the wind or do you have your back (or side) to it?

Photo 56 | *Be observant!*
A line of trees is just visible
in the distance. If it is windy,
you may be able to hear
them before you can see
them. If there is a breeze
blowing towards you, maybe
you can even smell them.

In mountain navigation terms, being observant means using all your senses, not just your eyes. One thing that all good navigators have in common is that they are keenly aware of their surroundings. Indeed, many people find that as they become more adept at navigation, their appreciation of landscape increases as they begin to perceive their surroundings in new, sometimes subtle ways.

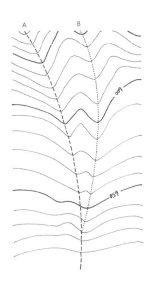

Figure 53 | *Parallel error.*
A = Intended route.
B = Actual route.

Be aware of gradient – does the land slope? If so, how steeply and in which direction? If you work out the fall line, you can measure the aspect of slope (as described in Chapter 15). You can then look on your map for places where there are slopes of a similar steepness and aspect.

Check your direction – if you tried to walk to the path or the objective without the aid of a compass, check the direction that you are now facing. It is extremely difficult to walk in a straight line in misty conditions without the aid of a compass, simply because, in the same way that we are either right- or left-handed, we are also either right- or left-footed – in other words, we all have a **dominant foot**! Your dominant foot is the one you would use if someone asked you to kick a football as hard as possible, and because most people take a slightly stronger stride with their dominant leg, there is a distinct possibility that they will veer to one side when trying to walk in a straight line. If you are right foot dominant, you will tend to veer to the left, and vice versa. This simple fact explains why people lost in the desert or jungle without a compass often tend to walk in large circles (see also Chapter 15).

Be aware of the potential for errors – particularly in poor visibility when it is easy to 'make things fit'; try not to make any rash assumptions. One small valley will look very much like every other small valley, and unless you are aware of the possibility of error, you can easily end up following the wrong feature (see Figure 53). This type of **parallel error** is one of the more common mistakes made in poor visibility. If you are travelling across terrain where there are few distinctive features, be aware not only of the potential for confusing one contour feature with another, but also of the implications of such a mistake.

Once you have gathered as much information as possible – some of it gleaned from thinking back over your journey so far, more of it obtained during your 360° sweep of the immediate area – face what you believe to be the most significant direction, set your map with your compass, then try to fit the information from the ground on to the 5% area of the map in which you know you must be located. If you can interpret your map to a reasonable standard, no matter where you are there will almost always be something you can identify, if not nearby then within reasonable striking distance. Look for combinations of features that will be instantly recognisable on the ground. For example, there may be a pool with a vertical face immediately to the north, and a stream running from the southern side with a waterfall a short distance downstream. Try to use combinations of features whenever possible – using features in isolation is rarely the best option.

Before you start going into a lot of detail, ask yourself whether you really need to know exactly where you are? Surely the bottom line is being able to use your navigation skills to escape from a potentially tricky situation, and this may mean simply being able to get to safety. In some circumstances, this may result in you ending up miles away from your car – but at least you are safe! And with the best will in the world, if you are standing in the middle of nowhere in thick mist and with no features anywhere in sight, there is very little you can do to pinpoint your position without either moving or using a reliable GPS device.

If you do find yourself 'temporarily mislocated' in the middle of nowhere and with a decreasing likelihood that you will be able to pinpoint your position, look for a linear feature on the map and then head towards it – it will act as a collecting feature which you can then use as a handrail to take you to a point where it is easier to work out your position. Having said this, you must think carefully about your options if it is so dark that you cannot see where you're going, or if you are in a potentially dangerous situation (e.g. near steep, rocky ground in thick mist or under winter conditions).

Example 2

In the second example, you are leapfrogging along a bearing to a pinpoint feature in thick mist. According to your watch, you are well over the time you estimated it would take you to get there, and your companion confirms that his pacing indicates that you have overshot the estimated distance by just over 100 metres. The temptation will be to carry on in the hope that your objective lies directly ahead only a few minutes away, but you must have the mental courage to stop, sit down and try to work things out logically.

First things first. As before, tell yourself that you are *not* lost – the last thing you need now is a brain made useless by panic. Think back along your route and try to remember any features you passed that might help you relocate yourself. Look at the ground within your range of visibility to see if that gives you any clues, and think about the nature and location of your objective. If, for example, your target is a stream junction, it will probably be located in a valley of some description. If, on the other hand, it is a trig point, it will often be on fairly high ground.

Photo 57 | *Don't only think about your target, but also about what lies around it.*

Do not look at your map yet – you cannot work out where you are by staring at a map. What you need is information from the ground, so slowly and deliberately turn round in a complete circle to get a 360° view of your surroundings, and glean as much information as you can. What is the vegetation like? What is the aspect and steepness of any slope? What is the shape of the land? Are there any features of any description in sight? If you believe it is safe to do so, you can extend your limit of visibility by sending a companion out to just within the limit of visibility. Once you have got as much information as possible, face what you consider to be the most significant direction, set your map with your compass, and try to fit the information you have gained from the ground on to the map.

Having done all this, if you are still as confused as before, carefully check all your calculations. Recalculate any estimates of time and distance, and confirm that the bearing set on your compass is the same as the one you thought you were following. If everything seems correct, recalculate the bearing from the map. If the bearing was taken from a route card drawn up the night before, you may have made an error when writing it up (a common mistake is forgetting to adjust for the magnetic variation). If you can still find nothing wrong, you will have to do one or more searches, as described in the last chapter. Remember to conduct these searches in such a way that you can always get back to your decision point, because in a situation like this, it is your only point of reference. If, on the other hand, you find that your time or distance estimations were incorrect or that you have been following the wrong bearing, work out where the error will have taken you, and then study the map to see if there are any definite features in that area which will help you relocate yourself.

Assuming that all your calculations are correct and that you have followed the bearing accurately, the likelihood is that you will find your objective during one of the searches. If not, keep calm. Ask yourself a series of questions. Did you start this leg of navigation from the correct point? If you started from a particular feature, were there any similar features nearby? For example, in misty conditions, one stream junction looks very much like another. If it is possible that you started from the wrong point, where would your bearing put you now? Are there are any identifiable features in that area that might help you relocate yourself? If not, what would happen if you continued along your present course? Are there any identifiable features on this course that might help you relocate yourself?

Is it possible that there might be a magnetic anomaly in the area? Does your compass needle point in the same direction as everyone else's? (When checking this, keep fairly well spread out because one compass will affect another.) Is it possible that your compass has been affected by something metallic or magnetic? Do you have a mobile phone in your breast pocket, or an auto-exposure camera hanging round your neck? Are you wearing a metallic watchstrap or an under-wired bra? Any of these could affect your compass enough to send you off course. If it appears that you may have been following the wrong bearing because your compass has proved faulty in some way, try to work out the rough direction in which you have been walking, but be careful when doing this because the error may not have been constant. Where does this new direction place you? Are there any identifiable features in that area that might help you relocate yourself?

If you know how far you have travelled (through either pacing or timing), you can draw a circle of that radius around the point from which you started. You should also have a rough idea of the direction in which you have travelled (even if it is the wrong direction!), so you should be able to choose a portion of the circumference to give you a rough location (see Figure 54). Are there any recognisable features on this part of the circumference of the circle that might help you relocate yourself?

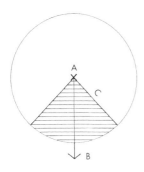

Figure 54 | *Time/distance*
circle.
A = Start point.
B = Approximate direction.
C = Approximate distance.

Is it possible that your map might be wrong? Is it possible that you may have interpreted the map incorrectly? Is it possible that the feature for which you were heading no longer exists? Trig points can be removed, field boundaries can be demolished, mountain pools can dry up, streams can change course, and paths can become overgrown. If this might have happened, does the shape of the land look right? And are there any other identifiable features in the area that might help you relocate yourself?

What should be obvious by now is that, no matter what the line of enquiry, you always end up asking about identifiable features. This is because the only way to locate yourself accurately in this situation is to find such a feature. There is simply no way you can pinpoint your position accurately if you are standing in the middle of nowhere in the mist, except (possibly) with a GPS device. If, however, you are standing by some type of feature and you think you can work out where you are, there is a simple way to confirm whether you are right or not, as follows.

First, using the map, look for a unique or readily identifiable feature (or combination of features) nearby – say within about two or three hundred metres. Second, work out a bearing and distance from your assumed current position to this feature or combination of features, and then pace along the bearing. If, after the set distance, you arrive at the feature or combination, you now know precisely where you are. If, on the other hand, you do not arrive at the feature or combination, turn around and return to the feature from which you started by pacing along a back bearing. At least you now know *where you are not*, and can mark it as such on the map! In navigation terms, knowing that you are definitely *not* somewhere is a positive!

If, after having asked all the pertinent questions and worked through all the possibilities, you are still totally confused and feel there is little hope of finding your target or relocating yourself, you will be forced to escape from the situation in some way. If you have been following a bearing up to this point, one option is to retrace your steps to your last known position using a back bearing. However, this will not always be the most suitable course of action, especially if this takes you further away from potential safety, or if you feel you may have deviated from the set bearing in some way.

If you have been following precise bearings and have kept your legs of navigation short, you should be able to work out your position to within, say, one kilometre. Even if you have been wandering aimlessly and have suddenly been overtaken by mist, you should still be able to judge your position to within a couple of kilometres at most. The next stage is to look at the map in order to find some form of long and well-defined linear feature that will lie across your path if you head towards it. This can be man-made (a road or a long field boundary, or the edge of a forest), or natural (a river or valley, a ridge, or a break of slope). You can even use a line of cliffs, but be aware that in any situation where you are unsure of your position, especially if the visibility is poor and even more so if you are in winter conditions when there may be cornices around, you should not head towards the *top* of a cliff. In fact, you should head in a direction that, if possible, avoids any potentially dangerous areas.

Referring back to Map 1, let us assume that you are 'temporarily mislocated' on the moors, somewhere in the region of grid square 1415. You had been heading for the trig point at 147159, but are now well overdue. You have searched but have found neither the trig point nor any sign of the path and line of cairns to the east of it, and the ground around you is so gently undulating as to make any aspect of slope readings almost meaningless. Having decided that there is little hope of finding the trig point, you look for an obvious escape feature that does not involve heading towards any potentially dangerous ground. If you head north, you will almost certainly find the break of slope where the moor descends into the valley (1416), but there is a line of outcrops shown just above the forestry, so you would need to take care. You could use this break of slope and then the outcrop as a handrail, turning right and following this to reach the northern side of the quarry (154169), and then east to the road at 156169. Alternatively, if you were to head either to the south or the west, you could be involved in a long trek before coming across anything positive, so walking in either of those directions would most likely be counterproductive. The obvious feature, however, is the road to the east, and reaching it involves you in no potential dangers (apart from, perhaps, the small quarry at 158162). No matter where you are on the moors, if you head in a generally easterly direction you will eventually reach the road.

Should you ever be unfortunate enough to find yourself in this type of situation, in worsening weather conditions and in an area that is ringed with potential dangers, you may well have to face the fact that the most advisable course of action is to find some shelter and sit it out – assuming, of course, that you are adequately equipped for such an eventuality. The ultimate responsibility is yours, and you will have to choose your course of action according to the factors affecting you at the time. Whatever you decide to do, try to keep calm and work through the problems systematically and rationally.

If you concentrate on what you are doing and double-check each move before you make it, there is a good chance that you will never find yourself in the unenviable position of having to face such a choice.

To recap

There is a definite sequence of events when you come to relocate. First and most important, stay calm! Second, resist the temptation to stare at the map – instead, take a good look at the ground around you, deliberately turning through 360°. Once you have got as much information as possible, face the direction you feel to be the most significant and use your compass to set your map. Finally, start putting the information you gathered from the ground onto the map.

Use searches if you believe your objective may be nearby, but if you have been following a bearing, always ensure that you can get back to it.

Double-check all your calculations, and if you find you have made a mistake, work out where that mistake will have put you on the map.

Once you believe you know where you are, confirm this if necessary by pacing along a bearing to a nearby feature or combination of features, found from the map.

There is no way you can pinpoint your position if you are standing in the middle of nowhere, so either try to find a definite feature (or combination of features) or look for a long linear feature which you can use as a handrail.

In the final analysis, if you cannot work out your position, you will have to find a way to escape, and this is best done by using collecting features such as handrails.

26 AND FINALLY ...

I cannot emphasise enough how important it is to practise your navigation skills before you need them for real. Indeed, you may be able to recite this book backwards, but unless you are both familiar and comfortable with the techniques I have described and have had practical experience of using them, your navigation will be less than effective. Potentially the biggest problem you will face is that when you need to be precise with your navigation, there will be a multitude of other things going on in your mind. If you are worried about your tired companions, your aching leg, the proximity of steep terrain, the dwindling time until dusk and the worsening weather, you will not want to struggle with a host of unfamiliar techniques – nor will you be able to do so effectively. So get out there and practise!

What I hope I have done in this book is describe a structured approach to navigation using simple, straightforward and effective techniques that can be used anywhere and in any conditions. As it happens, the details are unimportant! What is vital, however, is that you understand the underlying mechanisms – in other words, you need to have an appreciation of why you are doing what you are doing.

After over three decades of professional experience and some very memorable experiences (some of which, if I am honest, I would prefer to forget!), I believe I am just starting to become familiar with the techniques! Yet I still learn something almost every time I go into the wilder places, I still become 'locationally challenged' on regular occasions, and there are still times when I find it difficult to relate ground to map to ground. The big difference between now and when I started is purely one of confidence – I know that if I keep calm and work things out logically, I will be able to get myself to safety. But there is a huge difference between confidence and over-confidence, and navigation is only one part of the greater art of mountaincraft – albeit an essential one.

There is no such thing as an expert! With this type of navigation and with mountaincraft in general, you never know it all, and every trip is a potential learning experience. Different people will follow the same leg of navigation in totally different ways, yet will end up at the right place, so whenever you go out, try to learn from your companions.

The important thing is to go out there in the first place, to experience the wilderness, and to practise whenever you can. It is only 'by the doing' that you will learn.

Photo 58 | *The bottom line is getting back safely having had a good day.*

APPENDIX: PRACTICAL EXERCISE ANSWER

Description of the landscape shown on Map 4

Layer five

The outline shape is that of the head of a steep-sided valley running up from the south-east. The most prominent landscape feature in the grid square is an obvious break of slope at an altitude of about 600 metres, running north-south and bisecting the square. To the west of this break of slope, the angle is relatively gentle, whilst to the east it is extremely steep and is peppered with outcrops. Both these slopes face east. In the north-eastern corner of the square is the opposite side of the valley, and the slope here faces south-west. There is a corresponding break of slope here as well.

In more detail, the slopes above the break of slope (e.g. above 600 metres) are relatively smooth, whereas the valley sides below the break of slope are much steeper and concave (i.e. they are steeper at the top than at the bottom). Additionally, the western side of the valley is indented at its northern end by a significant tributary valley carrying a stream (264347). There is also another much smaller tributary valley (also carrying a stream) at the southern edge of the square (267340), with a very small dry gully immediately to its north (266341) – easy to miss unless you are using a magnifying lens.

Just north of the southernmost tributary valley is a significant rounded spur jutting into the valley from the west (268342). This is often missed because the contours are hidden beneath the black lines representing field boundaries. There is a slight flattening of the valley floor due north of this spur (268346) although the stream itself still runs in a tight bed, and there are also several very small undulations (shallow valleys and spurs) in this area, immediately east of the stream.

The west side of the valley, when viewed from the east, will appear dome-shaped, the highest part of the break of slope being almost in the centre of the square (265344), above and to the west of which the land gains height more gently. The highest part of the square is the extreme south-western corner (at just under 680 metres).

Layer four

The most obvious linear feature is the break of slope, already mentioned and clearly shown by the contours, the western portion of which is marked by a long line of outcrops. There is a stream which meanders from north to south along the floor of the valley, with a major tributary running from west to east (in its own valley), which meets the main stream in the northern part of the square (267347). This tributary valley has a line of outcrops curving along its southern edge, facing north to north-east. There are also several small outcrops in the base of the valley, facing east (267345 & 268344 – the latter partly hidden by the field boundary). There is also a smaller tributary at the southern edge of the square (as mentioned above), and a small line of outcrops facing north, running along the southern side of the very small dry gully to its north (266341).

There are several field boundaries shown in the south-eastern quarter of the square. Something that is often missed is the short, straight blue line which heads north-east towards the stream from where the two field boundaries on top of the spur meet (269342). This is, in fact, a mistake! It should actually be a black line, indicating a discontinuous field boundary leading down towards the stream. Minor mistakes on OS maps are actually quite common, and although I am led to believe that these are sometimes deliberate (as a way of catching unauthorised copying), the most common error is where the colours blue and black are confused during the scanning/printing process.

Other linear features include the paths, which are quite interesting in this square. Looking first at the green lines, there is a public bridleway shown running north-west to south-east along the northern side of the valley, and a public footpath which enters the square at 260344 (having left Offa's Dyke path which runs in the western adjoining square), heading straight as an arrow across the hillside and directly over the top of the outcrops! As mentioned in Chapter 5, green lines on maps do not necessarily indicate paths on the ground – they simply indicate where you have a right to walk. The symbol for a path on OS maps is a black 'pecked' (dashed) line, and if you look at the bridleway symbol running down the northern side of the valley, you will notice that there is also a black pecked line underneath it. Thus, a path was visible from the air when the map was surveyed, along which you can also legally walk or ride a non-motorised vehicle. There is no black pecked line underneath the public footpath symbol which leads over the top of the cliff, which means that no path was visible from the air when the map was surveyed. Indeed, there is no path visible even now (although you have a legal right to throw yourself over the edge!).

Finally, the extreme south-western corner of the square is crossed by a black pecked line – this is the actual route of Offa's Dyke path although the legal route is shown as being 150 metres further west in the adjoining square. The rights of way systems of Britain are strange indeed!

Layer three

There are few (if any) true pinpoint symbols in this square, although there are several things that can be used as pinpoint features. The most obvious are significant changes in the direction of the field boundaries, particularly where two boundaries join (the crossing of two linear features is often a very useful navigation feature), and the stream junction at 267347.

Layer two

The vegetation is mainly bracken, heath and rough grassland, with a concentration of bracken on the steeper, east-facing slopes below the rock outcrops. There are a few deciduous trees dotted around in the extreme south-eastern corner of the square, particularly around the small tributary valley followed by the non-existent public footpath.

Layer one

There is a community council boundary running from east to just north of west across the northern part of the square. The word 'Darren' in the central northern half of the square is a local name for a headland or truncated spur, and therefore refers to the rounded outcrop at 266348.

Please let me know if I have missed anything.

This area is shown in Photo 59, the photograph having been taken from the south-east, looking along a grid bearing of 287°.

Photo 59 | *A distant view of the area shown in Map 4 as seen from the south-east.*

GLOSSARY

Access land – land across which walkers have a legal 'right to roam'.

Aiming off – deliberately aiming to one side of an objective which lies on (or near) a linear feature.

Altimeter – an instrument which shows altitude.

Area symbols – symbols which indicate the characteristics of a large area, such as water and woodland.

Aspect of slope – the direction in which a slope faces.

Auxiliary contour – on Harvey/BMC maps, an additional contour showing the outline of a prominent physical feature that sits between the main contours and which would not otherwise be shown.

Back bearing – in this context, a bearing which points 180° away from your objective.

Base plate – the rectangular part of a compass, holding the magnifying lens, romer scales, and compass housing.

Boxing – avoiding an obstacle in a structured way by following a series of right angles (see Fig 28).

Break of slope – the line along which a slope changes angle from steep to shallow (or vice versa).

Cardinal points – the four main compass points: north, east, south and west.

Catching feature – a feature (or combination of features) just beyond your objective that alerts you if you have overshot.

Checking the quadrants – 'guesstimating' the angle of a bearing in order to confirm that it is heading in the right direction.

Chinagraph pencil – a soft, wax crayon that can be used to write on laminated maps, even in wet conditions.

Collecting feature – a feature or collection of features which lead you towards your objective.

Compass housing – the circular capsule on a protractor compass containing the compass needle.

Concave slope – a slope that becomes less steep as it descends (see also convex slope).

Contour lines/contours – lines on the map which indicate height, and thus show the shape of the land.

Conventional signs – the symbols on the map which indicate features on the ground.

Convex slope – a slope that becomes steeper as it descends (see also concave slope).

Dog-legging – avoiding an obstacle or hazardous area by following a bearing to an invisible point on the map before heading towards your objective (see Fig 29).

DOT arrow – the large arrow on the centre line of a compass that indicates your Direction of Travel.

Eastings – the vertical grid lines on maps which increase in value as you go east (see also northings).

Expanding spiral search – a search pattern that allows you to regain your original position if you do not find your objective.

Fall line – the line along which a ball would roll if the ground were completely smooth. This is always at right angles to the direction of the contours.

GPS – a gadget that give information based on Global Positioning System satellites.

Grid bearing – a compass bearing calculated using the grid lines on the map (see magnetic bearing).

Grid letters – the two letters which indicate from which 100km block a grid reference has been taken.

Grid lines – the series of horizontal and vertical lines on the map that allow you to give position coordinates and take accurate compass bearings. These are always exactly 1km apart, so can also be used to judge distance.

Grid north – the north point shown by the grid lines.

Grid reference – a series of 4, 6 or 8 figures (sometimes 10) that locate a feature on a map. The more figures there are, the more precise the location.

Grid squares – the squares on a map formed by the intersection of the grid lines.

Handrail feature – a long, linear feature such as a stream or field boundary, which can be easily followed.

Index line – the line on the compass housing where you read off your bearings.

Key – effectively, the map's dictionary.

KISS principle – one of the most important principles of successful navigation – Keep It Short and Simple!

Leapfrogging – following a compass bearing by sighting on your companions.

Line of sight – navigating by setting a map and looking at the landscape.

Line search – Approaching an objective in a line abreast in order to increase the visibility.

Linear feature – any feature that is long, such as a stream, valley, ridge, road, etc.

Magnetic anomalies – distortions in the earth's magnetic field resulting in errors when using compass bearings.

Magnetic bearing – a compass bearing calculated using the magnetic field of the earth, as shown by the compass needle (see also grid bearing).

Magnetic north – the north point shown by the compass needle.

Magnetic variation – the difference between grid north and magnetic north.

Magnetic zones – an arbitrary classification of regions of the earth where the lines of magnetic force point in different directions.

Micro-navigation – precision navigation using small features and short distances.

Mirror compass – a sighting compass containing a mirror to assist precise positioning of the compass needle over the orienting arrow.

Naismith's Rule – a formula which allows you to calculate how long it will take you to travel between two points.

National Grid – a system of numbered grid lines that allows you to pinpoint the position of any feature, anywhere in Britain.

Northings – the horizontal grid lines on maps which increase in value as you go north.

North-seeking – the red end of the compass needle that tries to point directly towards magnetic north.

Optical sighting compass – a protractor compass containing a prism that allows you to sight directly along a bearing.

Optimum time – the most likely time of arrival at your objective, as calculated using Naismith's Rule and a speed/time grid.

Orienting arrow – the arrow in the compass housing used to calculate and follow bearings.

Orienting lines – a series of parallel lines in the base of the compass housing used to calculate bearings.

Pace/distance grid – a table showing the effect of 5% and 10% errors when pacing different distances.

Pacing – counting paces in order to judge distance. In order to do this accurately, you need to know how many paces you take to cover a distance of 100 metres.

Parallel bearing – a bearing that runs alongside your intended course, but some distance from it.

Pinpoint symbols – a symbol on the map indicating anything that is small, isolated or instantly recognisable, the classic example (in the British countryside) being a trig point.

Protractor compass – any compass consisting of a rectangular base plate and a movable, circular compass housing.

Relocation – working out where you are when you think you are lost.

Resection – using two or more compass bearings to work out your position.

Ring contour – a small, circular contour indicating a local bump or hollow.

Romer scale – a scale that converts map distance into ground distance.

Rotational sweep search – a search pattern revolving around a central point.

Route card – a brief, written description of an intended route, including useful information such as bearings, distances and times, and often including one or more escape routes.

Rule of thirds – the way your eyes distort distances and heights when looking up or down slopes.

Scale – the ratio showing the difference between map distance and ground distance (e.g. 1:25,000 means distances on the ground are 25,000 times bigger than distances on the map).

Setting a map – turning a map in such a way that north on the map faces north on the ground.

Sighting compass – a compass containing either a mirror or a prism, which allows you to sight on features and follow bearings with great accuracy.

Speed/time grid – a table showing how long it will take to travel different distances at different speeds.

Spot height – a point on the map indicating a surveyed height above sea level.

Spotting – following a compass bearing by sighting on 'spots' on the ground.

Transit – when two or more pinpoint symbols are in line with one another, they are said to be in transit.

Tranter's Variations – a mind-bogglingly complex formula which attempts to make estimating time more accurate by taking into account such things as fitness and wind direction. It is rarely used.

Trig point – a small, concrete pillar, often at or near a summit, once used by the Ordnance Survey to calculate accurate distances and heights.

True north – the position of the geographic north pole.

Vertical interval – the difference in height between contour lines.

Waypoint – In the context of general navigation, any feature which is easily recognisable both on the map and on the ground, and which is readily visible over a reasonably long distance. In the context of GPS navigation, a location stored in the memory of a GPS device, either inputted by hand as a grid reference, or direct from a computer.

INDEX